CAMBRIDGE
Global English

for Cambridge Primary English as a Second Language

Workbook 5

Jane Boylan & Claire Medwell

Series Editor: Kathryn Harper

CAMBRIDGE
UNIVERSITY PRESS

University Printing House, Cambridge CB2 8BS, United Kingdom

One Liberty Plaza, 20th Floor, New York, NY 10006, USA

477 Williamstown Road, Port Melbourne, VIC 3207, Australia

314–321, 3rd Floor, Plot 3, Splendor Forum, Jasola District Centre, New Delhi – 110025, India

103 Penang Road, #05-06/07, Visioncrest Commercial, Singapore 238467

Cambridge University Press is part of the University of Cambridge.

It furthers the University's mission by disseminating knowledge in the pursuit of education, learning and research at the highest international levels of excellence.

www.cambridge.org
Information on this title: www.cambridge.org/9781108810890

© Cambridge University Press 2021

This publication is in copyright. Subject to statutory exception and to the provisions of relevant collective licensing agreements, no reproduction of any part may take place without the written permission of Cambridge University Press.

First published 2014
Second edition 2021

20 19 18 17 16 15 14 13 12 11

Printed in Malaysia by Vivar Printing

A catalogue record for this publication is available from the British Library

ISBN 978-1-108-81089-0 Paperback with Digital Access (1 Year)

Additional resources for this publication at www.cambridge.org/9781108810890

Cambridge University Press has no responsibility for the persistence or accuracy of URLs for external or third-party internet websites referred to in this publication, and does not guarantee that any content on such websites is, or will remain, accurate or appropriate. Information regarding prices, travel timetables, and other factual information given in this work is correct at the time of first printing but Cambridge University Press does not guarantee the accuracy of such information thereafter.

....

NOTICE TO TEACHERS
It is illegal to reproduce any part of this work in material form (including photocopying and electronic storage) except under the following circumstances:
(i) where you are abiding by a licence granted to your school or institution by the Copyright Licensing Agency;
(ii) where no such licence exists, or where you wish to exceed the terms of a licence, and you have gained the written permission of Cambridge University Press;
(iii) where you are allowed to reproduce without permission under the provisions of Chapter 3 of the Copyright, Designs and Patents Act 1988, which covers, for example, the reproduction of short passages within certain types of educational anthology and reproduction for the purposes of setting examination questions.

Contents

1 Talk about people

1.1	What are you like?	8
1.2	Adjectives and prepositions	10
1.3	The present simple	12
1.4	Role models	14
1.5	My favourite people	16
1.6	Check your progress	18
1.7	Reflection	19

2 Food and health

2.1	What are common illnesses?	20
2.2	Quantifiers	22
2.3	Modal verbs (advice and obligation)	24
2.4	Health blogs	26
2.5	Stone Soup, a world folktale	28
2.6	Check your progress	30
2.7	Reflection	31

3 Places

3.1	Where do you live?	32
3.2	Comparatives and superlatives	34
3.3	Past simple	36
3.4	Fictional places	38
3.5	*The Lost City*	40
3.6	Check your progress	42
3.7	Reflection	43

Contents

4 Special occasions

4.1	What celebrations and holidays are important in your country?	44
4.2	Defining relative clauses	46
4.3	Present continuous with future meaning	48
4.4	A traditional food	50
4.5	*Horrid Henry's Birthday Party*	52
4.6	Check your progress	54
4.7	Reflection	55

5 Our brains

5.1	Do you have a good memory?	56
5.2	Zero conditional	58
5.3	Tag questions	60
5.4	A report for a science investigation	62
5.5	*The girl who thought in pictures*	64
5.6	Check your progress	66
5.7	Reflection	67

6 Great stories

6.1	What's in a story?	68
6.2	Connectives	70
6.3	Past simple and past continuous	72
6.4	Lessons in life	74
6.5	*The Little Prince*	76
6.6	Check your progress	78
6.7	Reflection	79

Contents

7 Ancient civilisations

7.1	Why were these civilisations important?	80
7.2	Expressing opinions using *think, know, believe*	82
7.3	Imperative forms	84
7.4	An amazing discovery!	86
7.5	*Horatius at the Bridge*	88
7.6	Check your progress	90
7.7	Reflection	91

8 Rainforests

8.1	What do you know about rainforests?	92
8.2	The present perfect	94
8.3	Adverbs of degree	96
8.4	Rainforest animals	98
8.5	*A visit with Mr Tree Frog* and *If I were a sloth*	100
8.6	Check your progress	102
8.7	Reflection	103

9 Animal kingdom

9.1	Animal habitats	104
9.2	*It / Its*	106
9.3	Gerunds and infinitives	108
9.4	Animal rescue	110
9.5	*Mum won't let me keep a rabbit*	112
9.6	Check your progress	114
9.7	Reflection	115

How to use this book

This workbook provides questions for you to practise what you have learned in class. There is a unit to match each unit in your Learner's Book.

Tips to help you with your learning.

> **Writing tip**
>
> **Use paragraphs**
> Organise your essay into clear paragraphs: Location, Description, Opinion.

Information to help you find out more about grammar.

> **Language focus**
>
> **Adjective order**
> When we use more than one adjective to describe a noun, the adjectives need to be in the following order:
>
> | 1 | 2 | 3 | 4 | 5 | 6 | 7 | 8 | 9 |
> |---|---|---|---|---|---|---|---|---|
> | Number → | Opinion → | Size → | Shape → | Age → | Colour → | Origin → | Material → | Noun |
> | Three | fabulous | big | fat | old | brown | Costa Rican | furry | sloths |

Use the Cambridge Learner Corpus to get your grammar right!

> **Get it right!**
>
> Remember to use the present simple in both of the clauses.

Each Use of English session is divided into three parts:

Focus: these grammar questions help you to master the basics

> **Focus**
>
> 1 Read about a Carnival celebration and (circle) the correct words.
>
> **The Giants' Parade**
>
> Viareggio is a seaside town. The celebration ¹**which / who** they have along the seafront is colourful and fun. The artists show the papier maché giants ²**who / that** they have made specially for the parade. The people ³**who / which** take part dress up in the costumes ⁴**that / who** they have made and they cheer as the giants and floats pass by. The confetti ⁵**which / who** they throw is made of small, coloured pieces of paper. At night, the firework display ⁶**that / who** ends the celebration lights up the sky.

6

How to use this book

Practice: these grammar questions help you to become more accurate and confident →

Practice

2 Complete the sentences with *it* or *its*.
   a The zebra lives on the savannah. ___It___ has got black and white stripes. _____ stripes protect _____ from predators.
   b The kangaroo lives in herds in Australia. _____ uses _____ powerful legs to kick predators.
   c The giraffe is the tallest living land animal. _____ long neck helps _____ to reach the high leaves on the trees.

Challenge: these questions will help you use language fluently and prepare for the next level. →

Challenge ★

3 Interview your partner. Ask a question for each of these topics. Take notes.

   [family] [personality] [friend] [favourite things] [sports]

   Have you got any brothers and sisters?
   _____
   _____
   _____
   _____

Questions that cover what you have learned in the unit. If you can answer these, you are ready to move on to the next unit. →

> 5.6 Check your progress

1 Complete the sentences with the correct word.

   | reflexes sneeze brain neurons heartbeat yawn cerebellum brainstem |

   a We often _____ when we are tired.
   b A _____ travels very fast!
   c An average _____ for a 10-year-old is 84 beats per minute.
   d Do you have good _____?
   e The _____ controls your balance.
   f The _____ controls blood circulation.
   g _____ send information from the body to the brain.
   h The _____ has a left and a right side.

2 Circle the correct answer.
   a The brain weighs 1.3 kg, **does / doesn't** it?

Questions to help you think about how you learn. →

> 2.7 Reflection

Think about what you have studied in this unit. Answer the questions.

1 Which topics did you like and why?
   _____
   _____

2 Which activities did you like and why?

1 Talking about people

> ## 1.1 What are you like?

1 **Vocabulary: adjectives**

Find and (circle) these adjectives.

| cheerful quiet generous ~~hardworking~~ lazy nervous outgoing selfish shy |

H	A	R	D	W	O	R	K	I	N	G	G	W
C	H	A	P	T	D	S	V	A	O	H	E	Q
S	H	Y	Q	U	V	O	U	T	U	D	N	U
E	G	E	S	E	L	G	E	F	T	K	E	I
L	E	P	E	J	S	D	G	J	G	C	R	E
F	N	N	E	R	V	O	U	S	O	S	O	T
I	Y	D	A	V	F	J	P	N	I	E	U	P
S	L	A	Z	Y	S	U	O	M	N	L	S	H
H	S	A	T	H	A	R	L	D	G	A	Z	Y

2 **Complete these sentences with an adjective from Activity 1.**

a I've got a test today, so I'm feeling very ____nervous____.

b People say I'm very _____ because I'm always studying.

c My brother prefers watching the television to playing sport. He's so _____.

d My younger sister is very _____. She's got more friends than I have and she's only six!

e I'm very _____, but my friends aren't. They talk too much in class.

8

1.1 Think about it

3 Complete the words and match them to their opposite meaning.
   1 b_a_d-t_em_pe_r_ed
   2 __ hy
   3 s__lf__s__
   4 l __ z __
   5 c__lm
   6 qu__e__

   a generous
   b talkative
   c hardworking
   d nervous
   e outgoing
   f cheerful

4 Read the school report. Circle the picture of the boy described in the report.

   Juan has progressed quite well this year. He is a very polite, happy pupil and a very popular member of class. He works quite hard in class, but sometimes he talks too much with his classmates. His test marks aren't very good because he gets very nervous when we have an exam.

   a   b   c

5 Which adjectives in Activity 3 describe Juan's personality?
   _____

Challenge

6 Write sentences about your family using some of the adjectives in Activity 3. Give reasons why.

   My mum is very cheerful, because she's always singing!
   _____
   _____
   _____

1 Talking about people

> 1.2 Adjectives and prepositions

Use of English

Some adjectives are usually followed by a preposition. There are no grammar rules for these, so it's a good idea to learn them together. For example:

Adjective	Preposition
worried	about
interested	in
excited	about

I'm **worried about** climate change.

I'm **interested in** community projects.

I'm **excited about** my birthday party.

Focus

1 Read and circle the correct word in each sentence.

  a I'm ready **with / to** learn about how I can help protect the environment.

  b My friends and I are interested **in / about** animal protection.

  c We're excited **in / about** our school trip to the planetarium next Thursday.

  d I'm worried **of / about** my maths exam next week.

  e I'm shocked **by / with** the number of endangered species there are in the world.

  f I'm happy **in / about** the mark I got in my science project.

1.2 Use of English

Practice

Get it right!

Remember to use the correct preposition after an adjective.

I'm so happy **of** your visit next weekend. ✗

I'm so happy **about** your visit next weekend. ✓

2 Correct the five mistakes in Emma's journal entry.

> I'm worried ¹**in** people who have no home and have to sleep on the streets, so I was curious ²**of** my visit to the homeless shelter today. I was shocked ³**with** the number of people who sleep there every night. I took 100 blankets, which I collected last month, and gave them out to the people. They were pleased ⁴**in** the gift. I'm so happy ⁵**of** my community project and have plans to give out more blankets in the near future.

1 __about__   2 _____   3 _____   4 _____   5 _____

Challenge ★

3 Write sentences to describe how you feel about these topics. Use adjectives and prepositions from Activity 2.

- Your progress at school
- The destruction of the rainforests
- Your next holiday/school trip
- Climate change

I'm pleased with the mark I got in my English test.

_____
_____
_____
_____

1 Talking about people

> 1.3 The present simple

Use of English

Look at the present simple sentences. Which one is a state, a routine and a habit?

She **is** really outgoing and fun to be with.
I **have** lunch at half past one every day.
I always **play** tennis on Friday.

Remember the auxiliary verb in negative sentences!

My mum **don't** want me to go to bed late. ✗
My mum **doesn't** want me to go to bed late. ✓

Remember the auxiliary verb in questions too!

He live in Canada? ✗
Does he live in Canada? ✓
They like playing online? ✗
Do they like playing online? ✓

Focus

1 Circle the correct verb.

a Ahmed **have / has** a younger brother called Adam.
b He **likes / like** drawing and playing tennis.
c I usually **does / do** my homework in my bedroom.
d We always **play / plays** tennis at the weekend.
e She **think / thinks** she's good at speaking English.
f You **has / have** ten minutes to finish the exercise.

Get it right!

Remember to add the third person 's' to the verb.

He ~~do~~ **does** his homework after school.
She ~~get~~ **gets** up late at the weekend.

1.3 Use of English

Practice

2 Complete the dialogue with the correct verb.

Teacher: Hi Wei, how ¹____are____ you today?

Wei: ²_____ fine, thank you.

Teacher: Tell me about your family. ³_____ you got any brothers or sisters?

Wei: I ⁴_____ got an older sister. She ⁵_____ twelve.

Teacher: What ⁶_____ she like?

Wei: She ⁷_____ very outgoing and cheerful.

Teacher: What ⁸_____ you like doing?

Wei: I ⁹_____ painting and reading comics.

Teacher: ¹⁰_____ you like sport?

Wei: No, I ¹¹_____. I ¹²_____ not very good at it.

Challenge

3 Interview your partner. Ask a question for each of these topics. Take notes.

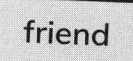 

family   personality   friend   favourite things   sports

Have you got any brothers and sisters?
_____
_____
_____
_____
_____

4 Write a report about the interview.

Adam has got two brothers ...

1 Talking about people

> 1.4 Role models

1 Read and match the headings to the paragraphs.

`Achievements`   `Background`   `Challenges and personality`   `An inspiration`

1 _____

Bethany was born on 8th February 1990 in Lihue, Hawaii. She has two older brothers. She got married in 2013 and has two young children.

2 _____

When she was 13 years old, a 4-metre-long tiger shark attacked her, biting off her left arm. She was rushed to hospital and she survived, despite losing 60% of the blood in her body. Bethany is a strong, determined and positive person, and one month after the attack she started surfing again.

3 _____

Two years later, Bethany won her first national surfing title! In 2004, she wrote her autobiography *Soul Surfer*, which was made into a major film in 2011.

4 _____

She is still a professional surfer and she is interested in helping other people in difficult situations. She has a blog, and she regularly gives motivational talks and courses to people all over the world.

2 **Read and answer the questions.**

a Circle one of Bethany's achievements since the attack.

b Why is it a miracle that she survived? Underline the information in the text.

c Find an example of an adjective + preposition. _____

d Find two examples in the present simple that express a state.
_____   _____

e Find an example in the present simple of a routine. _____

1.4 Write about it

3 Match these ideas to the headings about Natalie du Toit below.

South Africa

competing in the Paralympics

Andre du Toit (brother)

Age 14, lost her leg in a motorcycle accident

positive and determined

Won gold medals often gives motivational talks

'If I can achieve my dream, then anyone can!'

| Blog | Friends | Photos | Links |

Name: Natalie du Toit

1 Background South Africa,
2 Challenges
3 Personality
4 Achievements
5 Inspiration

Challenge

4 Write about Natalie using the notes in Activity 3 to help you.

Remember to use the present simple to write about states and routines.
Use some adjectives + prepositions.

1 Talking about people

> 1.5 My favourite people

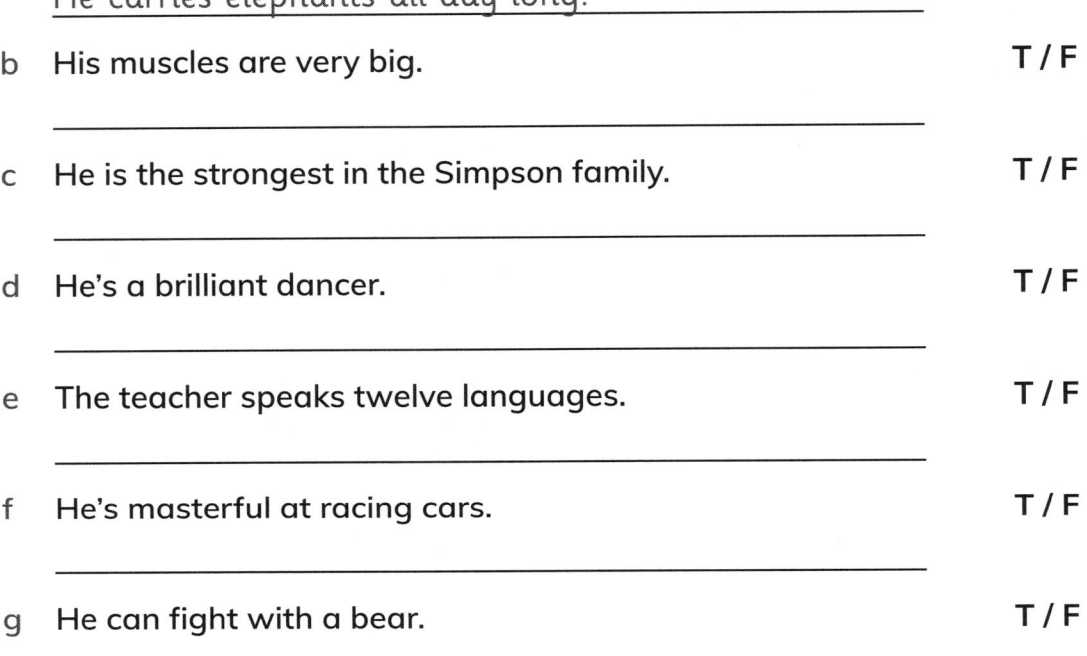

1 **Read** the poems *Our Teacher's multi-talented* and *Super Samson Simpson* in the Learner's Book again and (circle) if the sentences are true (T) or false (F). Correct the false sentences.

a Super Samson Simpson carries his grandma all day long.   T /(F)
<u>He carries elephants all day long.</u>

b His muscles are very big.   T / F
_____

c He is the strongest in the Simpson family.   T / F
_____

d He's a brilliant dancer.   T / F
_____

e The teacher speaks twelve languages.   T / F
_____

f He's masterful at racing cars.   T / F
_____

g He can fight with a bear.   T / F
_____

h He always combs his hair.   T / F
_____

2 **Vocabulary:** Complete the sentences with a word from the box.

| champion | wrestles | ~~dozen~~ |
| impressive | hoist | enormous |

Machine Man is the new superhero for kids. He can pick up a ¹_____ cars with one hand and ² <u>dozen</u> them in the air. His muscles are ³_____ and his legs are bionic, but these aren't his only talents. He's a ⁴_____ swimmer and he ⁵_____ with tigers. He also paints really ⁶_____ pictures, which are on display at the city gallery.

16

1.5 Read and respond

3 Complete Machine Man's profile.
Use information from Activity 2.

Physical qualities   Talents
___Bionic legs___   _____

_____   _____

_____   _____

4 Complete the poem about Machine Man.
Use the information from his profile.

Machine Man
His muscles _____,
His legs _____ too.
He's a champion _____,
And he _____ too.

5 **Values:** Think of a friend or family member. What are his/her personal qualities? Does he/she have any negative ones? What are his/her special abilities?

_____

_____

_____

Challenge ⭐

6 Write a short poem about a friend or a family member using the information from Activity 5.

_____

_____

_____

_____

17

1 Talking about people

> 1.6 Check your progress

Choose the correct answers and write in the space.

1 My brother is _____. He never shares anything with me!
   a generous   b lazy   c selfish

2 When my friend is _____ she bites her nails.
   a outgoing   b nervous   c bad-tempered

3 I am very _____ so I think I can pass the exam.
   a shy   b cheerful   c hardworking

4 I'm not very _____ on playing basketball.
   a quite   b keen   c like

5 We _____ like playing table tennis.
   a too   b bit   c both

6 I'm not _____ if I can go to the football match.
   a sure   b keen   c like

7 I'm really _____ about my birthday party on Saturday.
   a talkative   b lazy   c excited

8 Lucas is worried _____ the destruction of the rainforest.
   a in   b about   c of

9 I've got a dozen eggs! That's _____.
   a 12   b 10   c 13

10 She _____ like getting up early.
   a don't   b doesn't   c not

11 Habib is _____ at archery.
   a something of   b quite   c masterful

12 Luis won a gold medal in the swimming race. He's a _____ swimmer!
   a great at   b champion   c quite

> 1.7 Reflection

Think about what you have studied in this unit. Answer the questions.

1 Which topics did you like and why?

   _____

   _____

2 Which activities did you like and why?

   _____

   _____

3 What did you find challenging and why?

   _____

   _____

4 What help do you need now?

   _____

   _____

5 What do you want to find out more about?

   _____

   _____

2 Food and health

> ## 2.1 What are common illnesses?

1   Vocabulary: Sort the words. Write the symptoms next to the correct illness.

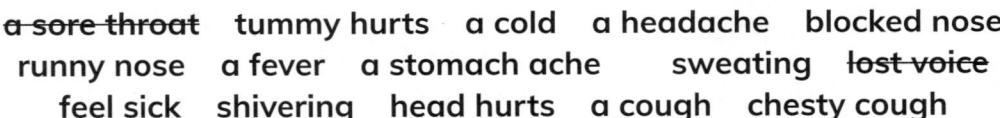

~~a sore throat~~   tummy hurts   a cold   a headache   blocked nose
runny nose   a fever   a stomach ache   sweating   ~~lost voice~~
feel sick   shivering   head hurts   a cough   chesty cough

Illness	Symptoms
a sore throat	lost voice

2   Read the dialogue and (circle) the correct indefinite pronoun.

Mrs Perkins: Hello, ¹(everybody)/ nobody.

Class: Hello, Mrs Perkins.

Mrs Perkins: Is ²anybody / everyone here? Ah! Has ³someone / anyone seen Khalid today?

Basim: ⁴No one / Nothing has seen him. He said ⁵something / no one yesterday about not feeling well. I think he had a stomach ache.

Mrs Perkins: Oh dear. OK – please get ⁶everything / something out of your bags.

2.1 Think about it

3 Complete the dialogues using the words from the box. Then match to the correct picture.

| head hurts   headache   ~~matter~~   sick |

a A: What's the ¹ __matter__ ?
   B: I've got a ² _____ .
   A: Do you feel ³ _____ ?
   B: No, only my ⁴ _____ .

| hot   sweating   fever |

b A: What's the matter?
   B: I feel ¹ _____ .
   A: Have you got a ² _____ ?
   B: Yes, I'm ³ _____ .

| sore throat   voice   fever |

c A: What's the matter? Have you got a ¹ _____ .
   B: No, I've got a ² _____ . I can't talk because I've lost my ³ _____ .

Challenge

4 Write your own dialogue. Use these prompts to help you.

| stomach ache   feel sick   no energy |

_____
_____
_____
_____

21

2 Food and health

> 2.2 Quantifiers

Use of English

Quantifiers are words that we use to show the amount of something. They can be used before countable and uncountable nouns.

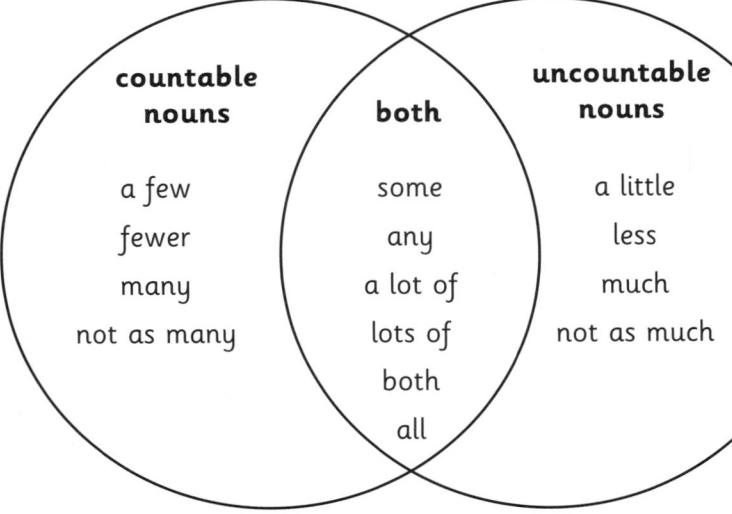

countable nouns	both	uncountable nouns
a few	some	a little
fewer	any	less
many	a lot of	much
not as many	lots of	not as much
	both	
	all	

You should drink **fewer** soft drinks.

Don't eat **as many** sweets because they are bad for you.

There is **less** sugar in dark chocolate than milk chocolate.

Focus

1 Circle the correct words in the sentence.

   a There is **a lot of / much** vitamin C in oranges.

   b We don't eat as **many / much** fruit as we should!

   c There are only **a few / less** vegetables left.

   d There is **fewer / less** cheese left in the fridge than I thought.

   e Dairy products provide us with **many / lots of** calcium, which is good for our bones.

   f Are there **some / any** soft drinks in the fridge?

2.2 Use of English

Practice

> **Get it right!**
>
> Think about whether the main noun is countable or uncountable in order to use the correct quantifier.
>
> We ate ~~many~~ *a lot of* delicious **food**.
>
> I didn't know that so ~~much~~ *many* **people** ate seafood.

2 Read the healthy eating blog and (circle) the correct quantifier.

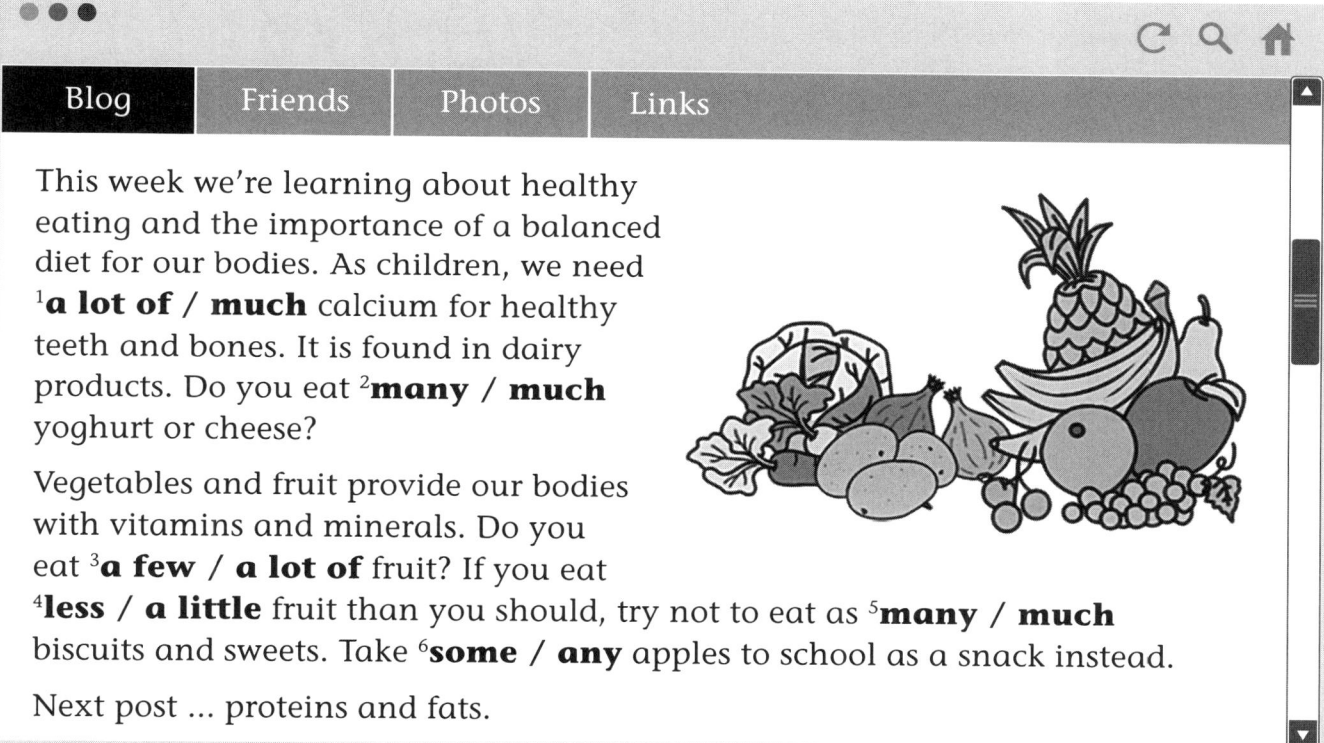

This week we're learning about healthy eating and the importance of a balanced diet for our bodies. As children, we need ¹**a lot of / much** calcium for healthy teeth and bones. It is found in dairy products. Do you eat ²**many / much** yoghurt or cheese?

Vegetables and fruit provide our bodies with vitamins and minerals. Do you eat ³**a few / a lot of** fruit? If you eat ⁴**less / a little** fruit than you should, try not to eat as ⁵**many / much** biscuits and sweets. Take ⁶**some / any** apples to school as a snack instead.

Next post ... proteins and fats.

Challenge

3 Complete these sentences for you about your diet. Use quantifiers.

   a I don't eat __a lot of__ sweets because they are bad for my teeth.

   b I drink _____.

   c I eat _____ fruit because _____.

   d I eat _____ vegetables because _____.

23

2 Food and health

> 2.3 Modal verbs (advice and obligation)

Use of English

We use the modal verb **should** to give advice.

You **should use** mosquito repellent when you travel to tropical countries.

You **shouldn't wear** shorts in the jungle.

We use **must** to express obligation.

You **must study** for the exam this evening.

You **mustn't touch** that it's very hot!

We use **need** to express obligation or no obligation to do something.

You **needn't take** off your shoes.

You **need to sleep** under a mosquito net.

Focus

1 **Put the words in the correct order.**

a to / You need / long trousers / wear / in the jungle
   You need to wear long trousers in the jungle.

b sleep / You needn't / a mosquito net / in England / under
   _____

c about malaria / You should / before travelling to tropical countries / read
   _____

d from insect bites / use / to protect ourselves / We must / insect repellent
   _____

e disturb / a bee's nest / mustn't / You
   _____

2.3 Use of English

Practice

2 Read the information about travelling to tropical countries. Circle the correct verb.

Get it right!

Don't forget to spell *mustn't* correctly.

You ~~musn't~~ mustn't arrive late to school.

Don't forget to *use* to after *need*.

~~You need eat more fruit.~~ ✗

You need to eat more fruit. ✓

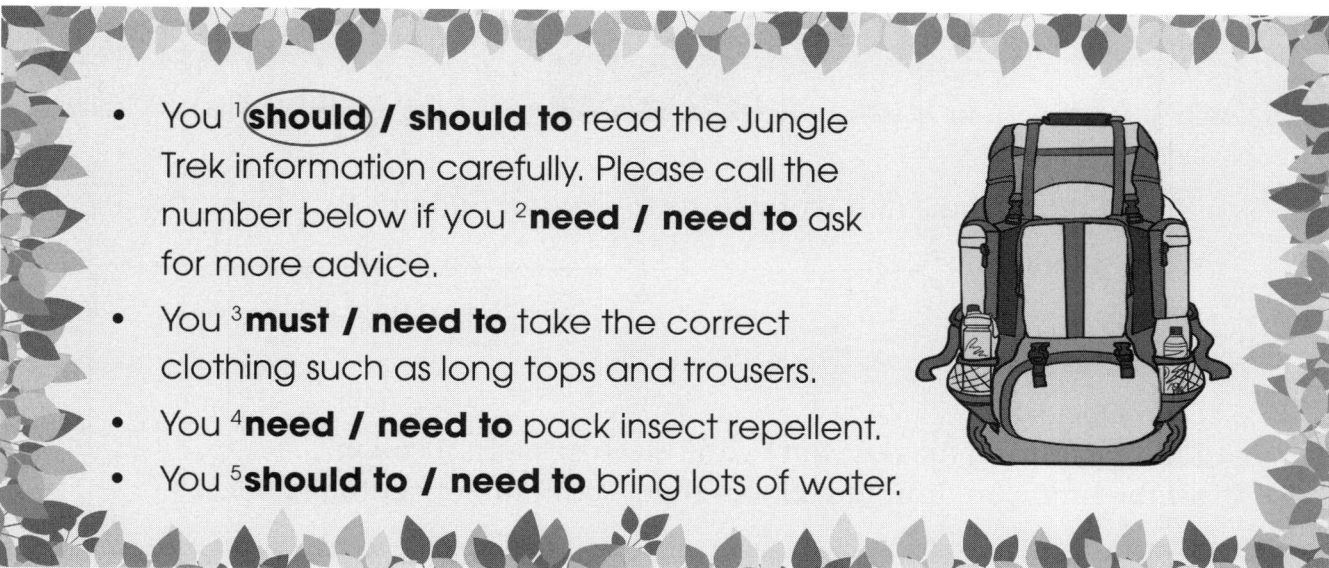

- You ¹**should** / **should to** read the Jungle Trek information carefully. Please call the number below if you ²**need** / **need to** ask for more advice.
- You ³**must** / **need to** take the correct clothing such as long tops and trousers.
- You ⁴**need** / **need to** pack insect repellent.
- You ⁵**should to** / **need to** bring lots of water.

Challenge

3 Imagine you are going on a trip with your school friends. Decide on a location (the mountains, the country, the coast). Write a list of things you need to take. Write sentences using modal verbs.

I need to take my sleeping bag.
___
___
___
___

25

2 Food and health

> 2.4 Health blogs

1 **Vocabulary:** Read and match the descriptions to the health problem.

> a sore throat   allergic reaction   stomach ache   chest infection

| Home | About | Services | **Blog** | Contact |

a Dear Doctor,
When I drink and eat, it really hurts to swallow and my neck hurts too.
What should I do? _____
Wei

b Dear Doctor,
I feel OK during the day, but I can't sleep at night. I cough all the time. I'm drinking a lot of fluids, but I'm not getting better.
What should I do? _____
Dan

c Dear Doctor,
Before I went to school this morning, I looked in the mirror and saw that I have red spots all over my arms, tummy and face. They are very itchy!
What should I do? _____
Ahmed

d Dear Doctor,
I came home from school this afternoon because after I ate my lunch, I started to feel sick. Now I don't feel sick, but my tummy hurts.
What should I do? _____
Mia

2.4 Write about it

2 Answer these questions with information from the blog.

a What symptoms does Wei have?
_____

b Why can't Dan sleep at night?
_____

c What is the problem with Ahmed's arms, face and tummy?
_____

d How did Mia feel after lunch?
_____

Challenge

3 Imagine you are a doctor. Write advice for one of the children with a health problem in Activity 1. Remember to use *should* and *shouldn't* to give advice.

| Home | About | Services | Blog | Contact |

_____

_____

_____

_____

_____

_____

_____

_____

2 Food and health

> 2.5 Stone Soup, a world folktale

1 **Read** the story *Stone Soup* again. Order the sentences a–j below, which summarise the story.

   a   On the day he ran out of money and food, he came across a village. ____

   b   The woman from the first house he had asked for some food gave him some mushrooms and herbs. ____

   c   No one in the village had any food at all. ____

   d   He knocked at the door of all the houses in the village asking for a little food. ____

   e   The young man told the elderly man that he wanted to make the villagers a big pot of soup from the special stone he had found on his travels because no one had any food. ____

   f   He asked the old man for a little onion and some cabbage. ____

   g   The elderly man gave him a large pot of water and a stirring spoon. __6__

   h   A little girl gave the young man a bowl of beans and some salt and pepper to put in the soup. ____

   i   Once there was a young man who was travelling around the country selling his goods. __1__

   j   Everyone had a delicious bowl of soup. ____

2 **Circle** the correct words.

   a   The villagers **had / didn't have** food.

   b   The stone **was / wasn't** magic.

   c   The villagers **wanted / didn't want** to help a stranger.

   d   The young man **persuaded / didn't persuade** the villagers to give him the ingredients for the soup.

   e   The young man **wasn't / was** very clever.

2.5 Read and respond

3 **Vocabulary: classifying expressions**

Label the food with the correct expression.

| a bag of   a pinch of   a bunch of   ~~a sack of~~   a head of   a bowl of |

a

a sack of potatoes

b

_____

c

_____

d

_____

e

_____

f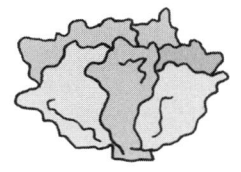

_____

4 **Values:** Circle the correct option for you.
  a I **always / sometimes / never** make my bed in the morning.
  b I **always / sometimes / never** recycle rubbish.
  c I **always / sometimes / never** give my seat to an elderly person on a bus.
  d I **always / sometimes / never** help my friends if they are upset about something.

Challenge

5 Write more examples of how you help others at home, at school or in your community.

_____

_____

_____

_____

2 Food and health

> 2.6 Check your progress

1 Match the sentence halves.

1 When I've got a cold …   a I sometimes lose my voice.
2 When I eat too much …   b I feel dizzy.
3 When I have a sore throat …   c provide our bodies with calcium.
4 When I have a fever …   d I usually have a runny nose.
5 When I have a headache …   e provide our bodies with protein.
6 Potatoes and rice …   f I shiver a lot.
7 Eggs, meat and fish …   g give us energy.
8 Dairy products …   h I feel sick.

2 Read and circle the correct answer.

> If you catch the flu you ¹**should / shouldn't** rest as much as possible. The symptoms you might have are headaches, a blocked nose and a fever. You probably won't have ²**any / less** energy to do all the things you usually do, and your body will hurt ³**a lot / many**. If you take ⁴**some / any** medicine, it will help you feel a bit better. You ⁵**should / shouldn't** eat ⁶**many / much** food if you have a fever, and be sure to drink ⁷**several / plenty of** fluids.

3 Complete these sentences about your diet.

a I usually eat _____ for breakfast.
b I always eat _____ for a snack.
c I never eat _____ for lunch.
d I sometimes eat _____ for lunch.
e I often eat _____ for dinner.
f I usually eat _____ before I go to bed.

Challenge

4 Write sentences in your notebook about the food you should and shouldn't eat in your diet and why.

> 2.7 Reflection

Think about what you have studied in this unit. Answer the questions.

1 Which topics did you like and why?

_____

_____

2 Which activities did you like and why?

_____

_____

3 What did you find challenging and why?

_____

_____

4 What help do you need now?

_____

_____

5 What do you want to find out more about?

_____

_____

3 Places

> 3.1 Where do you live?

1 **Vocabulary: Complete the words.**

a o _f_ _f_ i _c_ e b _u_ i _l_ d _i_ n _g_ s

b p _ _ e _ _ n _

c t _ _ f _ _ c l _ g _ _ s

d _ o _ p _ _ a _

e _ e b _ _ c _ _ _ s _ i _ g

f m _ u _ _ a _ n _

g _ a _ h

h f _ e _ _

i _ i _ e _

j f _ _ e _ t

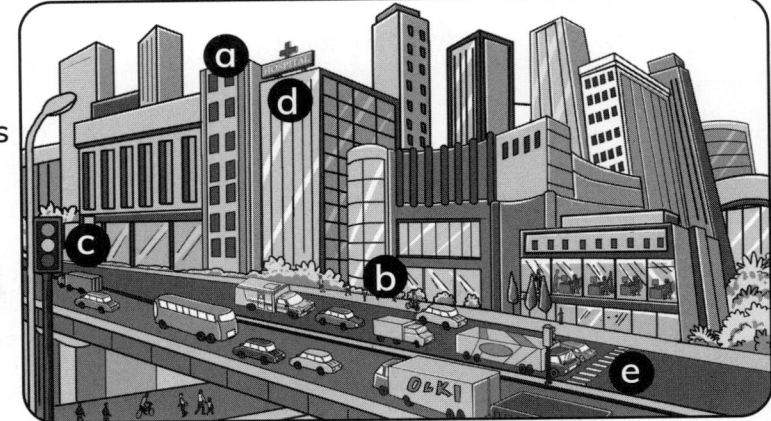

2 **Read the definitions and write the word.**

a Trees grow here. _forest_

b They are made of rock and they are very high. _____

c We walk along these in a city. _____

d This is where people can cross a road safely. _____

e We go here when we are very ill. _____

f Water flows in this. _____

3.1 Think about it

3 Circle the correct word to describe each picture.

a    b    c

an **ancient / noisy** building   an **ancient / amazing** view   a **busy / narrow** street

d    e

a **colourful / spectacular** building   a **peaceful / noisy** playground

4 Choose a word from Activity 3 to complete each sentence.

  a Living in the country is quiet and _____ .
  b Cities are very _____ places to live.
  c Cities have _____ streets full of people.
  d Trekking up to Machu Picchu is an _____ experience.
  e The view from the top of the Eiffel Tower is _____

Challenge

5 Write sentences using the adjectives in Activity 3 to describe where you live.

  I live in a noisy city.
  _____
  _____

3 Places

> 3.2 Comparatives and superlatives

Use of English

We use comparatives to compare things, and superlative adjectives to say which is at the top or bottom of something.

We add **-er** and **-est** for one syllable adjectives:

small – small**er** – small**est**

We add **-ier** and **-iest** for two syllable adjectives ending in y:

dirty – dirt**ier** – dirt**iest** (take away the y and use i instead)

We use **more** and **the most** with other two syllable (or more) adjectives.

crowded – **more** crowded – **the most** crowded

Comparatives and superlatives can also be used as adverbs:

He needs to cycle **faster** to win the race.

Everyone cycled fast, but Leo cycled **the fastest** in the race.

Watch out for irregular adjectives. They don't follow the rules!

good – better – the best

bad – worse – the worst

far – further – the furthest

Focus

1 Circle the correct word in each sentence.

    a   My city has the **more / most** spectacular street art in the world.

    b   My town is **further / the furthest** from the sea than the mountains.

    c   We need to look after the city parks **better / best**.

    d   I have **longer / the longest** journey to school in my class.

    e   The classroom next door is **the noisiest / noisier** than ours.

Practice

2 Read the text about visiting Buenos Aires in Argentina. Write the adjectives in brackets in their comparative or superlative form.

> **Get it right!**
>
> Don't use **more** or **most** with one syllable adjectives.
>
> My school is ~~more big~~ bigger than yours.
>
> It's the ~~most cold~~ coldest city I've ever visited.

ARGENTINA

Buenos Aires is one of Latin America's ¹ _largest_ (*large*) cities. It is near the east coast of Argentina and has a population of about 13 million. It is one of the ² _____ (*beautiful*) cities in Latin America, with great cafés and lovely buildings.

■ **Best time to travel**

If you are planning to visit Argentina, the ³_____ (*good*) time to go is in the autumn or the spring when the weather is good. In the winter it is ⁴_____ (*cold*) than in the autumn, and in the summer it's ⁵_____ (*hot*) and ⁶_____ (*humid*) than the other months of the year.

■ **Getting around**

Traffic in Buenos Aires is ⁷_____ (*heavy*) than in other Latin America cities, so you can travel around more quickly by either walking or using the metro, which is the ⁸_____ (*fast*) and ⁹_____ (*cheap*) way to travel.

■ **Things to see**

Don't leave Buenos Aires without going to Palermo Zoo to see the 300 animals. Or visit the Parque de la Costa, the ¹⁰_____ (*big*) amusement park in South America!

Challenge

3 Compare your city or town to Buenos Aires in Argentina. Use comparative and superlative adjectives.

<u>My city is smaller than Buenos Aires.</u>

_____

_____

3 Places

3.3 Past simple

Use of English

We use the past simple to talk about a past action, event or state that has finished. It is usually used with past time expressions, for example *yesterday, last night, two days ago, in the 1900s*.

I **walked** to school yesterday.

I **didn't have** an umbrella so I got very wet!

Did you walk to school yesterday?

Regular verbs end in **-ed** or **-d**.

Verbs ending in 'y' add **-ied**.

walk – walk**ed**   live – live**d**   try – tr**ied**

Remember to use the auxiliary verb **did** in yes / no questions, negatives and short answers.

Did you enjoy the party yesterday?   Yes, I **did**. / No, I **didn't**.

I **didn't enjoy** the party yesterday.

Focus

1   Complete the sentences with the correct form of the verb in brackets.

   a   I __didn't have__ (not have) a bicycle until I was five.

   b   In the 1980s, my dad _____ (walk) to school.

   c   One hundred years ago, families often _____ (live) all together in one house.

   d   People _____ (not use) mobile phones 40 years ago.

   e   In the past, children _____ (play) in the street more than they do now.

   f   My mum _____ (go) to a school in a nearby village when she was a child.

3.3 Use of English

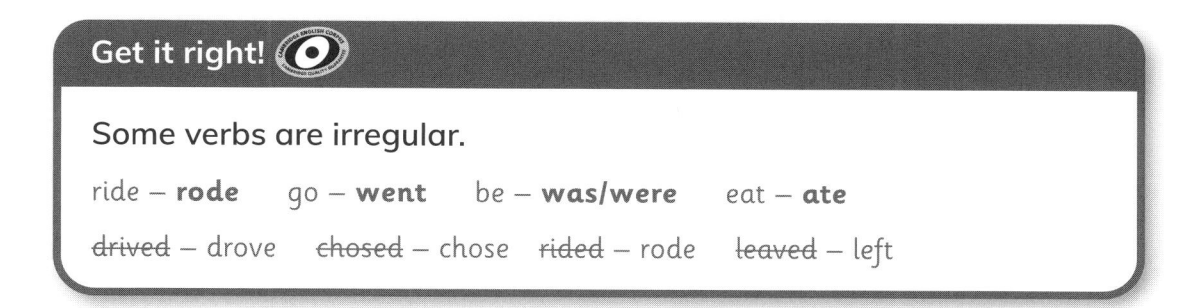

Get it right!

Some verbs are irregular.

ride – **rode**   go – **went**   be – **was/were**   eat – **ate**

~~drived~~ – drove   ~~chosed~~ – chose   ~~rided~~ – rode   ~~leaved~~ – left

Practice

2   Complete the text with the correct form of the verbs.

> not drive   walk   work   ride   not have (x 2)   not be   ~~live~~

In the past people ¹ __lived__ in houses with all the members of their family. The houses ² _____ running water or bathrooms. People often ³ _____ in the countryside in the fields, and they ⁴ _____ cars. They ⁵ _____ everywhere. To get around cities, people ⁶ _____ their bicycles. They ⁷ _____ the modern appliances we have today, and there ⁸ _____ any high-rise office buildings or apartment blocks.

Challenge ⭐

3   Write questions to ask an older family member about their childhood. Find out and write the answers. Ask questions about these objects.

telephone   microwave   dishwasher   car   computer

When my grandma was young, she didn't have a microwave or a telephone.

_____

_____

_____

3 Places

> 3.4 Fictional places

1 Read and match the description to the correct picture.

> Londorf is a dark, **scary** place at the end of the Earth. The only inhabitants of this **desolate** place are King Londorf, his army of beasts and a flock of **gigantic**, black crows.
>
> The dark clouds hide the light of the **pale** sun, and only the lava from the erupting volcanos lights up this dark, **miserable** place. The only other animals that survive in this place are **strange**, lizard-like creatures that live between the rocks and stones.
>
> I definitely wouldn't want to visit or live in this place, and I certainly wouldn't want to meet the army of beasts in King Londorf's castle!

a   b

Picture ☐

3.4 Write about it

2 Read the description again and answer these questions.

   a Which paragraph expresses the opinion of the writer? _____

   b Which paragraph talks about where Landorf is? _____

   c Which paragraph describes what Landorf is like? _____

3 Match the words in **bold** in the text to the words below.

   a sad   <u>miserable</u>   b unusual   _____

   c frightening _____   d very big   _____

   e a faint colour _____   f a bleak and lonely place _____

Challenge ⭐

4 Write about this fictional place. Invent a name.
   Choose interesting adjectives to describe it.

   | colourful   exotic   mysterious   gigantic |
   | strange   incredible   exciting |

Writing tip

Use paragraphs

Organise your essay into clear paragraphs: Location, Description, Opinion.

_____ (name of place) is _____.

There _____ and _____.

On the other side of the island there _____.

In the port, there _____.

3 Places

> 3.5 *The Lost City*

1 **Read *The Lost City* again and match each sentence to the picture it describes.**

1   2   3

4

a   'There it is! There is the Lost City! We have found it at last,' Ho-Shing said. __

b   'Look at their ruby eyes!' Yong-Hu said. 'Can I bang the gong?' __

c   Yong-Hu and Ho-Shing walked through the valley. 'I'm getting tired,' Yong-Hu complained. __

d   'We must climb these steps,' Ho-Shing said, pointing to very steep steps that led to the top of the wall. __

2 **Read and decide if these sentences are true (T) or false (F). Circle the correct answers. Correct the false sentences in your notebook.**

a   Yong-Hu and Ho-Shing are pandas. — **T** / F

b   Yong-Hu knows more about the Lost City than Ho-Shing. — T / F

c   There is a lot of bamboo in the Lost City. — T / F

d   It takes a day to walk to the Lost City. — T / F

e   Yong-Hu runs up all of the stairs in one go. — T / F

f   The music of the crickets is Yong-Hu's surprise. — T / F

3.5 Read and respond

3 **Vocabulary: Complete the sentences with the words from the box.**

| ~~chirp~~ | ruby | roar | reward | sparkle |

a Crickets and birds ____chirp____ .
b A _____ is a precious red stone.
c The music of the crickets was the _____ for their journey.
d A _____ is the sound a lion makes.
e The roofs of the buildings _____ in the sunshine.

4 Answer the questions about the story.

a Why does Ho-Shing want to find the Lost City?
   _____

b What do they hear on the way?
   _____

c How long does it take them to get there?
   _____

d What is special about the roofs of the buildings?
   _____

e What did the pandas find in the Lost City?
   _____

Challenge ⭐

5 **Values: Look at the pictures and write about the ways in which we can look after our environment in your notebooks.**

41

3 Places

> 3.6 Check your progress

1 Complete the crossword.

Across →

4 You walk on this alongside a road or street.

5 When you are ill you might go here.

9 The opposite of dirty.

10 Animals are often kept in these in the countryside.

Down ↓

1 When there are a lot of people in a place.

2 A lot of trees in a group.

3 When something looks frightening.

6 Very quiet.

7 Very old.

8 Very big.

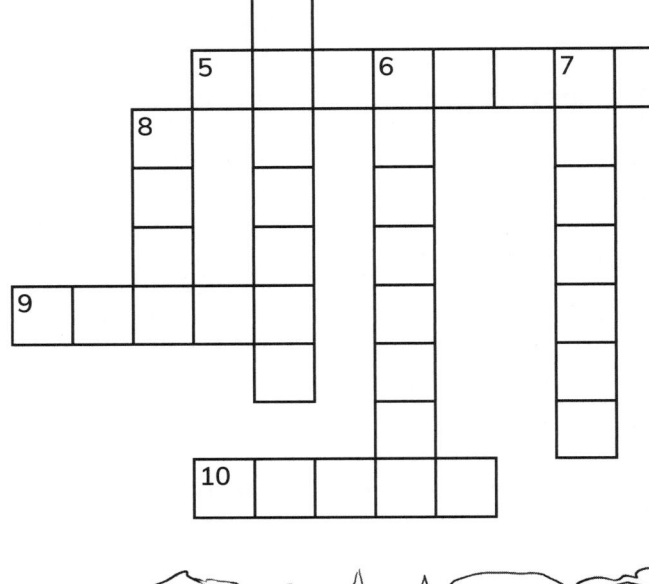

Challenge ⭐

2 Make a revision crossword to test your friends!

3.7 Reflection

Think about what you have studied in this unit. Answer the questions.

1 Which topics did you like and why?

_____

_____

2 Which activities did you like and why?

_____

_____

3 What did you find challenging and why?

_____

_____

4 What help do you need now?

_____

_____

5 What do you want to find out more about?

_____

_____

4 Special occasions

> 4.1 What celebrations and holidays are important in your country?

1 **Vocabulary:** Find and circle the celebration words.

F	D	S	L	I	G	H	T	S	S	K	P
I	L	C	J	H	Y	D	G	E	P	P	A
R	A	S	Y	M	B	O	L	Z	Y	U	R
E	N	D	J	W	B	D	D	Z	B	D	A
W	T	E	Z	X	N	F	E	A	S	T	D
O	E	Q	G	A	J	K	P	H	I	Y	E
R	R	F	C	C	O	S	T	U	M	E	S
K	N	E	X	O	E	V	N	U	E	Q	B
S	S	J	R	P	G	W	I	U	H	C	K
D	E	C	O	R	A	T	I	O	N	S	H
P	D	G	T	Q	V	N	V	B	Y	V	M
F	H	C	X	T	V	R	D	S	C	C	E

~~lights~~
fireworks
feast
decorations
parades
lanterns
candles
symbol
costumes

2 **Complete the sentences with a word from Activity 1.**

a The _fireworks_ display is brilliant on New Year's Eve! They light up the night sky and make lots of noise.

b There were lots of delicious traditional dishes on the table. What a _____!

c A dragon is a _____ of Chinese New Year celebrations.

d During the festival we hang beautiful _____ from the windows of our houses.

e The carnival _____ through the streets of Rio de Janeiro are the most spectacular in the world.

f Diwali is the 'Festival of Lights', so we light _____ in our house.

4.1 Think about it

3 Read the text and complete the table about the festival.

> The colourful festival of Holi is celebrated at the end of February or early March and lasts for a day. Holi has an ancient origin and celebrates that 'good' is better than 'bad'. Holi celebrations begin with lighting a bonfire on the Holi Eve. On the day of Holi, people spray coloured water on each other with *pichkaris* (water pistols). The most enjoyable tradition of Holi is the tradition of breaking the pot. A pot of buttermilk is hung high above the street. Men form a huge human pyramid and the man on the top breaks the pot with his head. People also eat traditional things like *thandai* (a drink) or *pakoras* (fried vegetables) and they hug and wish each other 'Happy Holi'.

Name of festival	When is it celebrated?	What does it celebrate?	How long does it last?	How do people celebrate it?
Holi				

Challenge

4 Complete the diagram with information about a festival you celebrate. Draw a picture of a symbol, a decoration, food or drink to illustrate it.

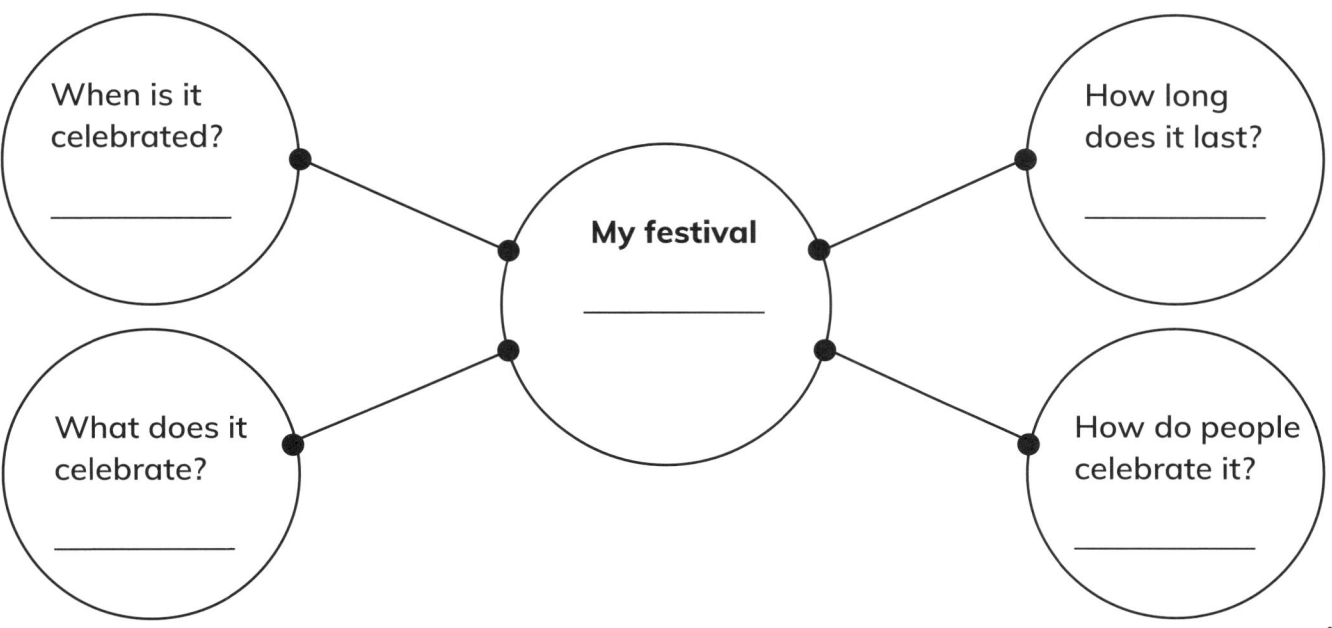

- When is it celebrated? _____
- How long does it last? _____
- What does it celebrate? _____
- How do people celebrate it? _____

My festival _____

45

4 Special occasions

> 4.2 Defining relative clauses

> **Use of English**
>
> We use defining relative clauses to give us important information about people and things.
>
> A defining relative clause tells us which person or thing the speaker means.
>
> We can use who or that to talk about people.
>
> The school children are gymnasts **who** perform in the parade.
>
> We use that or which to talk about things.
>
> Lanterns are decorations **that** we hang in our windows.

Focus

1 **Read about a Carnival celebration and circle the correct words.**

The Giants' Parade

Viareggio is a seaside town. The celebration ¹**which / who** they have along the seafront is colourful and fun. The artists show the papier maché giants ²**who / that** they have made specially for the parade. The people ³**who / which** take part dress up in the costumes ⁴**that / who** they have made and they cheer as the giants and floats pass by. The confetti ⁵**which / who** they throw is made of small, coloured pieces of paper. At night, the firework display ⁶**that / who** ends the celebration lights up the sky.

4.2 Use of English

Practice

> **Get it right!** 👁
>
> **Don't forget the relative clause!**
>
> ~~He's the cook made the delicious food.~~ ✗
>
> He's the cook who made the delicious food. ✓

2 Complete each sentence with the correct defining clause.

a They are the lanterns _____ we hang in our windows.

b They are the boys _____ dance through the streets with the dragon.

c Venice is the other city _____ has a big carnival celebration.

Challenge ⭐

3 Design and describe your own giant for a Carnival parade. Draw a picture.

_____
_____
_____
_____
_____
_____
_____
_____
_____
_____

4 Special occasions

> 4.3 Present continuous with future meaning

Use of English

We use the present continuous to talk about plans that you have organised in the future.

We're **meeting** Sara at 4 p.m. on Friday.
I'm **having** a pyjama party with my friends at the weekend.

Questions

Are you having a party tomorrow? Yes, I am. / No, I'm not.
Is he travelling here by car tonight? Yes, he is. / No, he isn't.

Focus

1 Complete the sentences with the correct form of the verb.

   a My friends ___are arriving___ at 12 p.m. today.
   b They _____ (travel) by train to the celebration tomorrow.
   c We _____ (cook) traditional food for the party at the weekend.
   d Children _____ (bring) the hats they have made to the parade today.
   e I _____ (have) my friends over for a party when I've finished lunch.

4.3 Use of English

> **Get it right!**
>
> Don't forget to add the auxiliary verb *be*.
>
> ~~She~~ *She's* staying at her friend's house tomorrow.
>
> **Spelling**
>
> Remove the **e** on verbs that end in **e**.
>
> come > coming
>
> With verbs that end in consonant-vowel-consonant, double the last letter.
>
> sit > si**tt**ing

Practice

2 Match the plans to how they were organised.

1 We're flying to Venice on Saturday.
2 We're watching the latest *Star Wars* film tonight at the cinema.
3 Mum is helping me make cookies later.
4 I'm helping my friend with his English revision.
5 I'm going to the park later to play football with my friends.

a We have tickets for 6 p.m.
b We're meeting in the library this afternoon.
c We've booked a hotel on the Grand Canal.
d We agreed to meet at 4 p.m.
e We bought the ingredients this morning.

Challenge ⭐

3 Complete these sentences for you. Use the present continuous to talk about your plans.

a I _____ tonight.
b I _____ tomorrow.
c I _____ on Thursday.
d I _____ at the weekend.

49

4 Special occasions

> 4.4 A traditional food

1 Read and match the photos to the descriptions.

1 In Ghana, they celebrate the yam harvest with the festival of Homowo, which lasts for three days. A yam looks a bit like a potato, but it is longer and more pointed. It's a very important crop in Ghana, and many special foods are made from it, such as mashed yams with boiled eggs.

A

2 In Korea, they give thanks to the harvest during Chu Suk with a special feast. Families prepare *Songphyun*, which are rice cakes made of rice, beans, sesame seeds and chestnuts. Women sing and dance, and they also play a game called turtle tag.

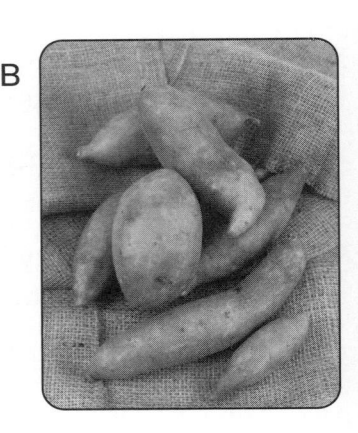

B

2 Complete the sentences with the correct words.

| made from | called | lasts | celebrates |

a The yam harvest Homowo _____ for three days.

b Special foods are _____ yams.

c They eat a special dish _____ *Songphyun*.

d Chu Suk _____ the harvest with a special feast.

4.4 Write about it

3   Find and <u>underline</u> these nouns, adjectives and verbs in the descriptions in Activity 1.

   a   a comparative adjective (paragraph 1)

   b   two types of food (paragraph 1)

   c   two action verbs (paragraph 2)

   d   a game (paragraph 2)

   e   the ingredients for *Songphyun* (paragraph 2)

Challenge ★

4   Use the notes below to write about Trung Thu, a Vietnamese festival.

Name of festival	Trung Thu
What does it mark?	The harvest moon
A traditional food	Moon cakes (made of salted eggs, seeds, vegetables and oil)
How do they celebrate?	Colourful masks Parade with different shaped lanterns

Writing tip

Useful language

It's called …

It celebrates …

It marks the end of / beginning of / the arrival of …

It's made of / with …

4 Special occasions

> ## 4.5 Horrid Henry's Birthday Party

1 **Read *Horrid Henry's Birthday Party* again. Why doesn't Henry want these classmates to come to his party?**

   a Margaret   _Because she's too moody._
   b Susan   _____
   c Andrew   _____
   d Toby   _____
   e William   _____
   f Ralph   _____

2 **Unscramble the adjectives and match them to the classmates they describe on Henry's list. Use the text on pages 70–71 in the Learner's Book to help you.**

Invitation list

Clever Clare   _____ Andrew
Moody Margaret   _____ Ralph
_____ Toby   _Jolly_ Josh
_____ William   _____ Graham

~~veclre~~
nxosuai
erdu
gohtu
eweyp
regyed

3 **Decide which sentences are fact (F) or opinion (O). Circle the correct answer.**

   a Andrew is no fun.   (F) / O
   b I don't want any girls at all, thought Henry.   F / O
   c He crossed out Moody Margaret's name.   F / O
   d Ralph didn't invite Henry to his party.   F / O
   e He didn't want Peter to come to his party.   F / O
   f No horrid kids would be coming to his party.   F / O
   g No guests meant no presents.   F / O

4.5 Read and respond

4 **Read the clues and do the crossword.**

Down ↓

1 Someone who is fun.
4 Someone who is not polite.
5 Someone who doesn't work hard.
6 Someone who is strong.

Across →

2 Someone who is bad-tempered.
3 Someone who is intelligent.
7 Someone who is nervous.
8 Someone who cries a lot.

5 **Vocabulary: Write the opposite adjectives.**

a The giant wasn't weak. He was big and ___tough___.
  He could lift up a car with one hand.

b The boy is not polite: in fact, he is _____.
  He never says *please* or *thank you* to anyone.

c He isn't confident. He gets very _____ when he has an exam.

d She's always angry and she never smiles. She's _____.

e She's such a _____ person. She's always smiling.

f He's so _____. He's always studying at his desk.

> tough   anxious
> bad-tempered
> hard-working
> rude   jolly

Challenge ⭐

6 **Values: Write about three people you value (a family member, a friend, a teacher).**

Think about their positive characteristics, for example kindness, generosity.

a I value my _____ because _____.
b I value my _____ because _____.
c I value my _____ because _____.

4 Special occasions

> 4.6 Check your progress

Choose the correct answers and write in the space.

1 On New Year's Eve there are _____ displays in public places.
   a lights   b firework   c lantern

2 A dragon _____ through the streets during the Chinese New Year celebrations.
   a rides   b flies   c parades

3 The Rio de Janeiro Carnival _____ for four days.
   a celebrates   b lasts   c takes place

4 A costume is something _____ people wear during a celebration.
   a who   b that   c where

5 Tourists _____ come to watch the Carnival are amazed!
   a who   b that   c which

6 I _____ a party for my 18th birthday.
   a have   b 'm having   c having

7 She _____ her friend in the shopping centre this afternoon.
   a meets   b meeting   c is meeting

8 I received a lovely _____ from my friend on my birthday.
   a food   b eggs   c gift

9 We _____ a special song at our spring festival.
   a get   b make   c sing

10 William is so _____. He cries all the time!
   a weepy   b clever   c anxious

11 Your son needs to be more polite in class. Sometimes he is very _____.
   a miserable   b lazy   c rude

12 She can be very _____ at times. She sits in her room and won't speak to anyone.
   a moody   b cheerful   c hard-working

> 4.7 Reflection

Think about what you have studied in this unit. Answer the questions.

1 Which topics did you like and why?

   _____
   _____

2 Which activities did you like and why?

   _____
   _____

3 What did you find challenging and why?

   _____
   _____

4 What help do you need now?

   _____
   _____

5 What do you want to find out more about?

   _____
   _____

5 Our brains

> 5.1 Do you have a good memory?

1 **Try this short-term memory experiment.**

   1 Look at the pictures below for 30 seconds.
   2 Then cover up the pictures.
   3 Write the words you can remember.
   4 Uncover the pictures and check your answers

chocolate	road	bread	forest	cheese
field	pasta	hospital	sweets	river

2 **Now try this experiment! Follow the same instructions as in Activity 1.**

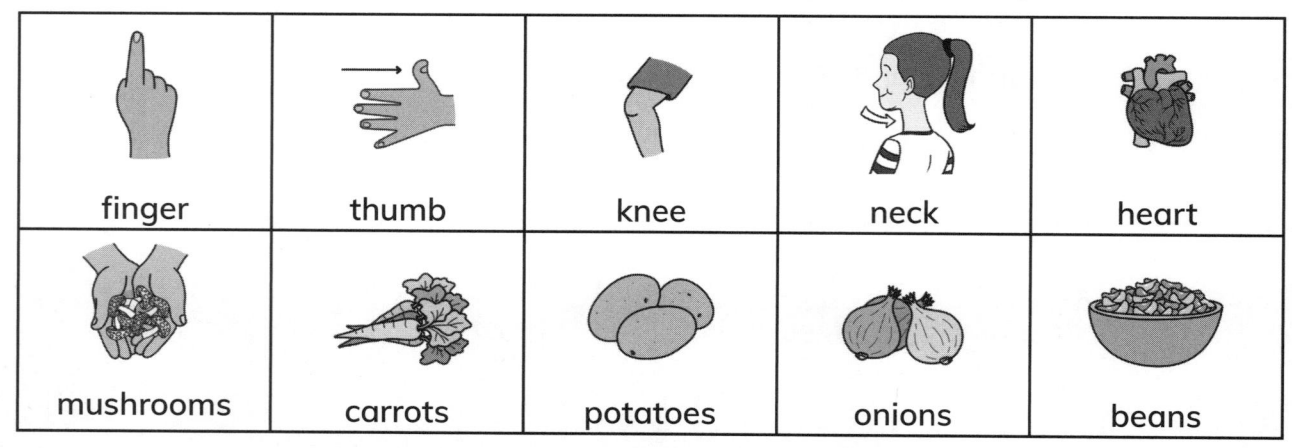

finger	thumb	knee	neck	heart
mushrooms	carrots	potatoes	onions	beans

Solution: If you could remember seven or more that's excellent! Your short-term memory is very good. If you could remember between five and seven, that's OK too. If you could remember fewer than five, you need to work on your memory techniques! If you did better in Activity 2 that's because the words were grouped in topics, which helps our brains remember better. Use this technique for remembering vocabulary.

5.1 Think about it

3 Complete the text with the words in the box.

> heartbeat   reflexes   hitting   sneezing   hot   pull   yawning

Brain power

A reflex is an involuntary action that your body does in response to something. Our brain controls involuntary actions, which means we don't have to think to make them happen. For example, if you touch something ¹_____, your brain makes you ²_____ your hand away fast. The part of the brain that controls this is called the medulla. Other involuntary actions include ³_____ when we are tired or ⁴_____ when we have a cold or an allergy to something. It also controls our ⁵_____. A doctor can check the ⁶_____ in your knee by ⁷_____ them gently with a small hammer. The reflexes in your knees are important for keeping your balance.

Challenge ⭐

4 An eye experiment: Why do our pupils change size?
Read and follow the instructions.

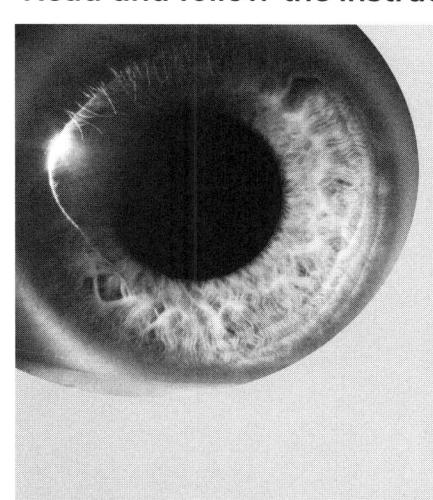

In a light room, look in a mirror and note the size of your pupils (the black spots in the middle of your eyes). Now go to a dark room for one minute or turn off the lights. Return to the light room and look at the size of your pupils. Have they changed in size?

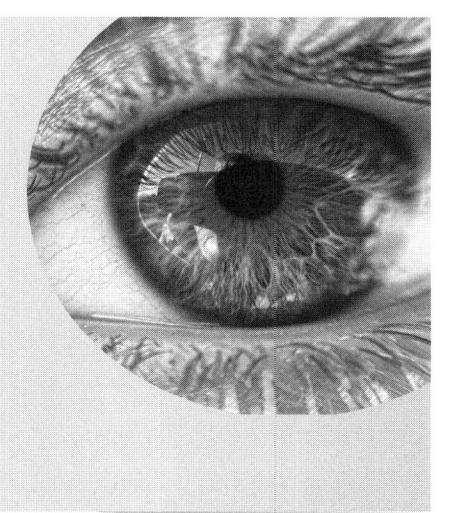

Your pupils should get smaller to protect your eyes from too much light.

5 Our brains

> 5.2 Zero conditional

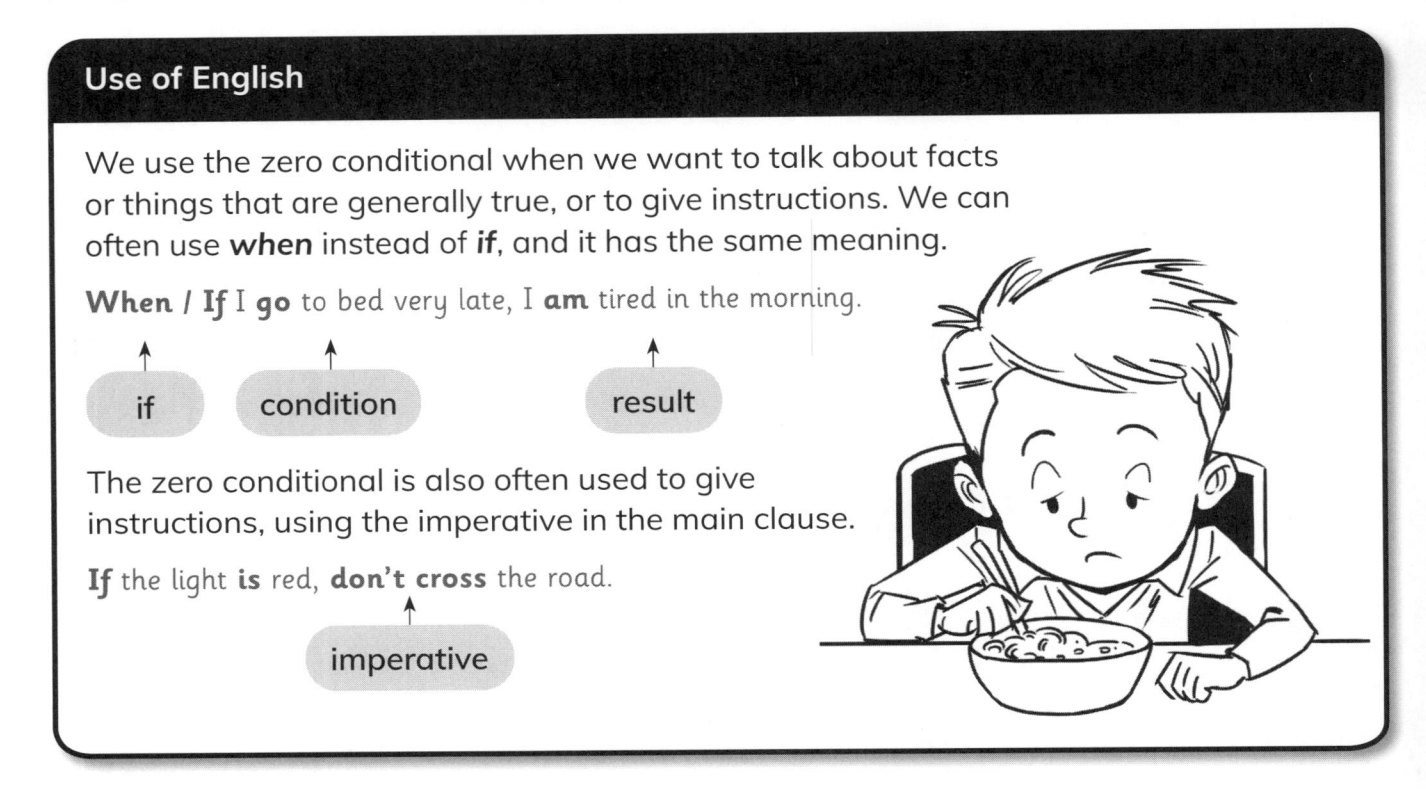

Use of English

We use the zero conditional when we want to talk about facts or things that are generally true, or to give instructions. We can often use **when** instead of **if**, and it has the same meaning.

When / If I **go** to bed very late, I **am** tired in the morning.

↑ if   ↑ condition   ↑ result

The zero conditional is also often used to give instructions, using the imperative in the main clause.

If the light **is** red, **don't cross** the road.
↑ imperative

Focus

1 **Match and make zero conditional sentences.**

1 If you press the button, …
2 When you run fast, …
3 If you want a healthy brain, …
4 When you hear the school bell, …
5 If you see a swarm of bees, …
6 If you ride your bike to school, …

a your heart beats faster.
b go straight to your class.
c stay calm.
d the video game starts.
e eat lots of fruit and vegetables!
f wear your helmet.

5.2 Use of English

Practice

2 Complete these general truths using the zero conditional. Use the pictures to help you.

Get it right!

Remember to use the present simple in both of the clauses.

a If I don't eat breakfast, ... (get / hungry)

_____

_____

b If I'm late for class, ... (teacher / get angry)

_____

_____

c When the sun goes down, ... (get dark)

_____

_____

d If you eat an ice cream in the sun, ... (melt quickly)

_____

_____

Challenge ⭐

3 Complete these sentences for you. Use the zero conditional.

a When I'm happy, I _____.

b When I'm sad, I _____.

c When I'm tired, I _____.

d When I'm hungry, I _____.

5 Our brains

> 5.3 Tag questions

Use of English

- We use tag questions to check information we already know or think we know.
- Remember, if there is an auxiliary verb in the sentence, we use it to form the question tag.
- If the sentence is positive, add a negative tag.
- If the sentence is negative, add a positive tag.

Playing music **is** good for the brain, **isn't** it?

You **don't** know how to juggle, **do** you?

Sometimes there is no auxiliary verb already in the sentence. So, we use **don't**, **doesn't** or **didn't**.

Harry **likes** pizza, **doesn't** he?

You **saw** her last week, **didn't** you?

Focus

1 **Complete the sentences with the correct tag question.**

   a The left side of the brain **is** better at problem solving, ____isn't it____?

   b The right side of the brain helps us to understand music, _____?

   c The brain has three main parts, _____?

   d The cerebrum is bigger than the cerebellum, _____?

   e Pizza isn't good brain food, _____?

   f The brain stem connects to the spinal cord, _____?

   g Juggling can't make your brain stronger, _____?

5.3 Use of English

Practice

2 Complete this dialogue about what's good for the brain. Use tag questions.

Monia: Do you look after your brain, Ahmed?

Ahmed: Well, I do a lot of **exercise**. That's good for the brain, ¹_____?

Monia: I don't think your diet is important, ²_____?

Ahmed: Oh, I think a **healthy diet** is really important!

Monia: I tried **juggling** the other day. It makes your brain stronger, ³_____?

Ahmed: I don't know, but Omega 3, which we get from **fish** like salmon, is good ⁴_____?

Monia: Yes, it is. **Wearing a helmet** when you ride your bike also protects your brain, ⁵_____?

Ahmed: Yes, I definitely agree with you on that.

Get it right!

Remember to use the correct auxiliary verb for the tag question.

You are good at maths, ~~do~~ **aren't** you?

He likes learning English, ~~isn't~~ **doesn't** he?

Challenge ⭐

3 Write your opinion about the words in bold in the dialogue. Use expressions to share your opinion.

a I agree with Ahmed that exercise is good for the brain.

b _____

c _____

d _____

e _____

5.4 A report for a science investigation

1. Read the report about Wei's memory experiment.
   Put the stages (A–D) in order and number them 1–4.

   Name: Wei

   Project title: A memory experiment

   Objective: To test our short-term visual memory.
   To find out how many objects I can remember in one minute.

   Materials: 10 or more classroom objects such as a pencil, pen, ruler, rubber, pen drive, notebook, textbook, etc. …

   Stages:

   A _____, uncover the objects and compare to the list to see how many I remembered. ☐

   B _____, put all the classroom objects on a table or a tray. Look at the objects for 20 seconds. ☐

   C _____, cover the objects with a cloth or a piece of card. ☐

   D _____, write a list of all the objects I can remember. ☐

   Results: I discovered that I have a good visual memory. I remembered nine out of ten objects. The one I didn't remember was the pencil sharpener.

   Conclusion: To conclude, in my opinion this is a fun experiment to test your memory!

2. Complete the report with these sequencing words.

   > finally   after that   then   first

3. How does Wei give her opinion in the report?

4. What do you think of Wei's experiment? Give your opinion.

   _____
   _____

5.4 Write about it

5 Can you s-t-r-e-t-c-h your brain?
   Are you better at remembering numbers or words?
   Do this experiment.

   79, 8, 101

   diet brain sneeze

   Stage 1: Look at the numbers in the box for 20 seconds. Then cover them up. Write down as many as you can remember. Uncover to check.

   | 3 | 256 | 79 | 8 | 15 | 101 | 52 | 21 |

   Stage 2: Look at these words for 20 seconds. Then cover them up. Write down as many as you can remember. Uncover to check.

   | brain | exercise | digestion | cerebrum | spinal cord | diet | helmet | sneeze |

6 Now complete the experiment report sheet with your results and conclusion.

   Writing tip

   Reporting language

   ... to find out ...
   We discovered that ...
   First, then, finally ...
   To conclude ...
   In my opinion, ...

   Name: _____

   Project title: _____

   Objective: Do I remember numbers or words better?

   Materials: _____
   _____

   Stages: First, _____
   _____

   Then, _____

   After that, _____

   Finally, _____
   _____

   Results: I discovered that _____

   Conclusion: To conclude, in my opinion _____

5 Our brains

> 5.5 The girl who thought in pictures

1   Read *The girl who thought in pictures* again.
    Find three adjectives that describe Temple's personality.

    _____   _____   _____

2   Think of three adjectives to describe your personality.
    Are you similar to Temple in any way?

    I'm hardworking because I study a lot.
    _____
    _____

3   Vocabulary: Match these words to the correct pictures.

    | a twirled | b tag | c shrieked | d hug | e itch |

    1   2   3   4   5

4   Complete these sentences using a word from Activity 3.

    a   They gave each other a big _____.

    b   He _____ when the monkey jumped on the table.

    c   The little boy _____ around until he was dizzy.

    d   The cat's flea bites made him _____.

    e   She tried to pull the _____ off her new dress.

5.5 Read and respond

5 Complete these sentences about Temple's likes and dislikes.

a She loves _____.

b She hates _____.

6 Complete these sentences using a word that rhymes with the word in bold.

> hooray   towns   hug   twirled   away

a What did she **say**? She said, 'Go _____!'

b What a wonderful **day** to celebrate, _____!

c The little **girl** danced and _____ across the stage.

d He didn't like the loud **sounds** of traffic and people in bustling _____.

e The baby tugged and **tugged** until he got a _____.

7 Read and complete the second verse of the poem with the rhyming words.

> see   town   sounds   agreed

The girl ...
Who liked to twirl,
Woke up one day
'It's sunny, come on,
Let's dance and play.'

She twirled her way across the [1]_____,
And listened to all the lovely [2]_____.
Everyone came out to clap and [3]_____,
'What a talented dancer,' they all [4]_____

8 Write your own short poem in your notebook. Use rhyming words.

9 Values: How can you be kind and caring towards your classmates? Tick the pictures you agree with.

a

b

c

65

5 Our brains

> 5.6 Check your progress

1 Complete the sentences with the correct word.

| reflexes   sneeze   brain   neurons   heartbeat   yawn   cerebellum   brainstem |

a We often _____ when we are tired.
b A _____ travels very fast!
c An average _____ for a 10-year-old is 84 beats per minute.
d Do you have good _____?
e The _____ controls your balance.
f The _____ controls blood circulation.
g _____ send information from the body to the brain.
h The _____ has a left and a right side.

2 Circle the correct answer.

a The brain weighs 1.3 kg, **does / doesn't** it?
b It doesn't control our emotions, **doesn't / does** it?
c Breathing is controlled by the brain stem, **isn't / is** it?
d Your heart **beat / beats** faster if you do exercise.
e If you touch something sharp, you **pulled / pull** away your hand fast.
f If you **yawn / yawned** in class, you are either tired or bored.

Challenge

3 Complete these sentences with your ideas about things you have learned in this unit.

a The most amazing thing about the brain is _____.
b If you have a good short-term memory, _____.
c I can look after my brain power by _____.
d If you play a musical instrument, _____.

> 5.7 Reflection

Think about what you have studied in this unit.
Answer the questions.

1   Which topics did you like and why?

    _____

    _____

2   Which activities did you like and why?

    _____

    _____

3   What did you find challenging and why?

    _____

    _____

4   What help do you need now?

    _____

    _____

5   What do you want to find out more about?

    _____

    _____

6 Great stories

> ## 6.1 What's in a story?

1 **Vocabulary:** What types of books are they?

Complete with these words. There is one extra word.

| picture | family | ~~board~~ | comic | tales | novels | fables |

a   ~board~ book

b   _____ book

c   superhero _____

d   _____ stories

e   _____

f   fairy _____

2 Match the definitions to types of stories using the wordpool in Activity 1.

1 Stories about families, which are passed down from parents to children. _d_

2 These are thick, hard books for babies. __

3 These are full of small, action pictures with some text under each picture. __

4 Stories with a moral and often have animals as characters. __

5 Stories with pictures and no text. __

6 Stories told to children that usually have a happy ending. __

6.1 Think about it

3 Ayesha is interviewing Amal about her reading habits. Complete the dialogue with words from Activity 1.

Ayesha: When did you start reading books, Amal?

Amal: Well, when I was about six months old, I liked looking at the pictures of animals in thick ¹_____. I used to point to them and say their names. When I was older, I liked reading ²_____. They had no words, but my parents told the stories to me.

Ayesha: So, when did you start reading words in books?

Amal: When I was about five. I loved reading ³_____ with my parents at bedtime. One of my favourites was *Snow White*. I also liked it when my family told me ⁴_____ about things that happened to them when they were young.

Ayesha: What do you like reading now?

Amal: Well, now I prefer reading ⁵_____. I'm reading one about young detectives at the moment, and it's really good! I'm also reading ⁶_____, which are stories about animals that teach us a moral.

Challenge ⭐

4 Interview a person in your family about their reading habits. Take notes in your notebook.

5 Write about his/her reading habits, using these expressions to help you.

> When he/she was about …   When he/she was older …
> One of his/her favourites was …   Now, he/she likes reading …

_____
_____
_____
_____

6 Great stories

> 6.2 Connectives

Use of English

We use connectives to join parts of a sentence. Words like **and**, **after**, **but**, **so**, **when** and **next** are connectives.

They add information:
I went into the library **and** took the biggest, oldest book off the shelf.

They express time and sequence:
Next, I put it on the table and opened it.
When I turned the first page, I saw a picture of an ancient tribe.

They express results:
It looked interesting, **so** I turned another page.

They contrast information:
There was a map, **but** it wasn't very clear.

Focus

1 Read another story about the Cool detective gang. Circle the correct connective.

The Cool Detective Gang heard the alarm bells of their local museum ring during the middle of the night, ¹ **so / but** they decided to get up ² **and / after** go out to investigate. The police still hadn't arrived ³ **when / next** they got to the museum, ⁴ **so / but** they decided to look around the outside. Suddenly, they heard a loud noise. It was a window breaking. They ran towards the noise ⁵ **and / after** hid behind a bush. ⁶ **Next / And** they saw the thief running away with a painting under his arm. Lily stuck out her foot when the thief was running past their hiding place, ⁷ **and / but** he fell to the ground. ⁸ **But / After** the police arrived, they took the thief to the police station.

6.2 Use of English

Get it right!

Remember to use the correct connective.

I'm free next Saturday ~~and~~ we can go to the cinema. ✗

I'm free next Saturday **so** we can go to the cinema. ✓

Practice

2. Read the beginning of a story about the deadly serpent of Koshi and complete it with the connectives.

| when | and | but | so |

The deadly serpent of Koshi was no ordinary serpent. It had eight heads ¹_____ eight tails. It was enormous and could be seen from many kilometres away. One day, the villagers saw it moving towards their village, ²_____ they ran to hide in nearby caves, ³_____ one person didn't hide – a famous knight. ⁴_____ the serpent was almost upon the village ...

Challenge ⭐

3. How do you think the story of the deadly serpent of Koshi ends? Use your imagination to write the ending of the story. Use connectives to link your ideas.

When the serpent was almost upon the village ...

_____

_____

_____

6.3 Past simple and past continuous

Use of English

When we use the **past simple** and the **past continuous** together in a sentence, a **long action** (past continuous) is interrupted by a **short action** (past simple).

Last summer, I **was walking** along the beach when I **saw** a dolphin!

long action — short action

We use connectives like when, while and as to join the parts of the sentence.

I took a photo of the dolphin **as** it was leaping out of the sea.

Focus

1 Complete these sentences using the past simple or the past continuous of the verb in brackets.

   a The girl ___was drawing___ (draw) a picture when her mum _____ (call) her.

   b The wind _____ (blow) the newspaper out of Mum's hands as she _____ (read) it.

   c Alice _____ (read) a book when her friend _____ (text) her.

   d The family _____ (leave) the hotel room when the young girl _____ (see) something strange.

6.3 Use of English

> **Get it right!**
>
> Remember to use the past continuous!
>
> ~~When she **walked** along the street, she **found** some money on the pavement.~~ ✗
>
> When she **was walking** along the street, she found some money on the pavement. ✓

Practice

2 Read and complete the anecdote with the past simple and past continuous.

Yesterday, I ¹ _was walking_ home from school singing my favourite song when I ² _____ (hear) a strange sound. The sound ³ _____ (came) from behind a bush. As I was tiptoeing toward the bush, I ⁴ _____ (sneeze) and a kitten ⁵ _____ (run) out from behind the bush. It looked scared, so I picked it up and put it inside my coat. As I ⁶ _____ (go) home it ⁷ _____ (fall asleep) inside my coat. Mum ⁸ _____ (cook) when I arrived home, and I asked her if I could keep it. She said, 'Yes!'

Challenge ⭐

3 Use your imagination and complete these sentences as if you were writing your own anecdote. Use the past simple and the past continuous.

a I was swimming in the sea when _____.

b I saw a strange creature as _____.

c I was walking in the park when _____.

d I heard a strange noise as _____.

e I was falling asleep when _____.

6 Great stories

> 6.4 Lessons in life

1 Read these proverbs from around the world and match them to the pictures.

> 1 Practice makes perfect.
>
> 2 Think before you speak.
>
> 3 Many hands make light work.

a   b   c

2 Match the meanings to the proverbs from Activity 1.

   a We need to keep trying at things if we want to be good at them.

   b If we all work together the work is easier.

   c Think about what you are going to do before you do it.

3 **Punctuate these missing sentences from the story on page 75.**

   a You'll just have to stay there until you get thin again

   b Where am I going to find something to eat he cried to himself

   c Marvellous he said

   d Tee-hee-hee

6.4 Write about it

4 Read and complete the story with the sentences from Activity 3.

It was a cold winter's day, and Felix the Fox was walking through the forest. He was very hungry.
1 _____

As he passed a big oak tree, he could smell something delicious. Inside a hole in the trunk was some bread and meat that a man had left there. Felix crept inside, and he ate and he ate and he ate.
2 _____ licking his lips when he'd finished the very last bit, but when he tried to get out of the tree, he couldn't! His tummy was so full! He squeezed … and he squeezed … but it was no good. He was stuck.
3 _____ laughed a bee buzzing past.
4 _____ And by the time Felix got out, he was as hungry as before!

5 Read the story again. Which proverb from Activity 1 does it match?

_____

Challenge ⭐

6 Now write your own short story based on one of the proverbs in Activity 1. Before you start writing, brainstorm ideas for your story.

a Where is the setting for the story?
b Describe the setting.
c Who are the characters?
d What are they doing?
e Is there a problem?
f How is the problem solved?
g What is the outcome/resolution?

6 Great stories

> 6.5 The Little Prince

1   Read this summary of the story.
    Circle the correct answers to complete it.

> The Little Prince came to Earth because he had been having some trouble with ¹**the king / a flower**. When the Little Prince arrived on Earth he met a ²**snake / flower** in ³**Asia / Africa**. Then he crossed the ⁴**city / desert**, where he met a ⁵**flower / tree**. Finally, he climbed a ⁶**mountain / tower** to see the whole planet and the ⁷**animals / people**.

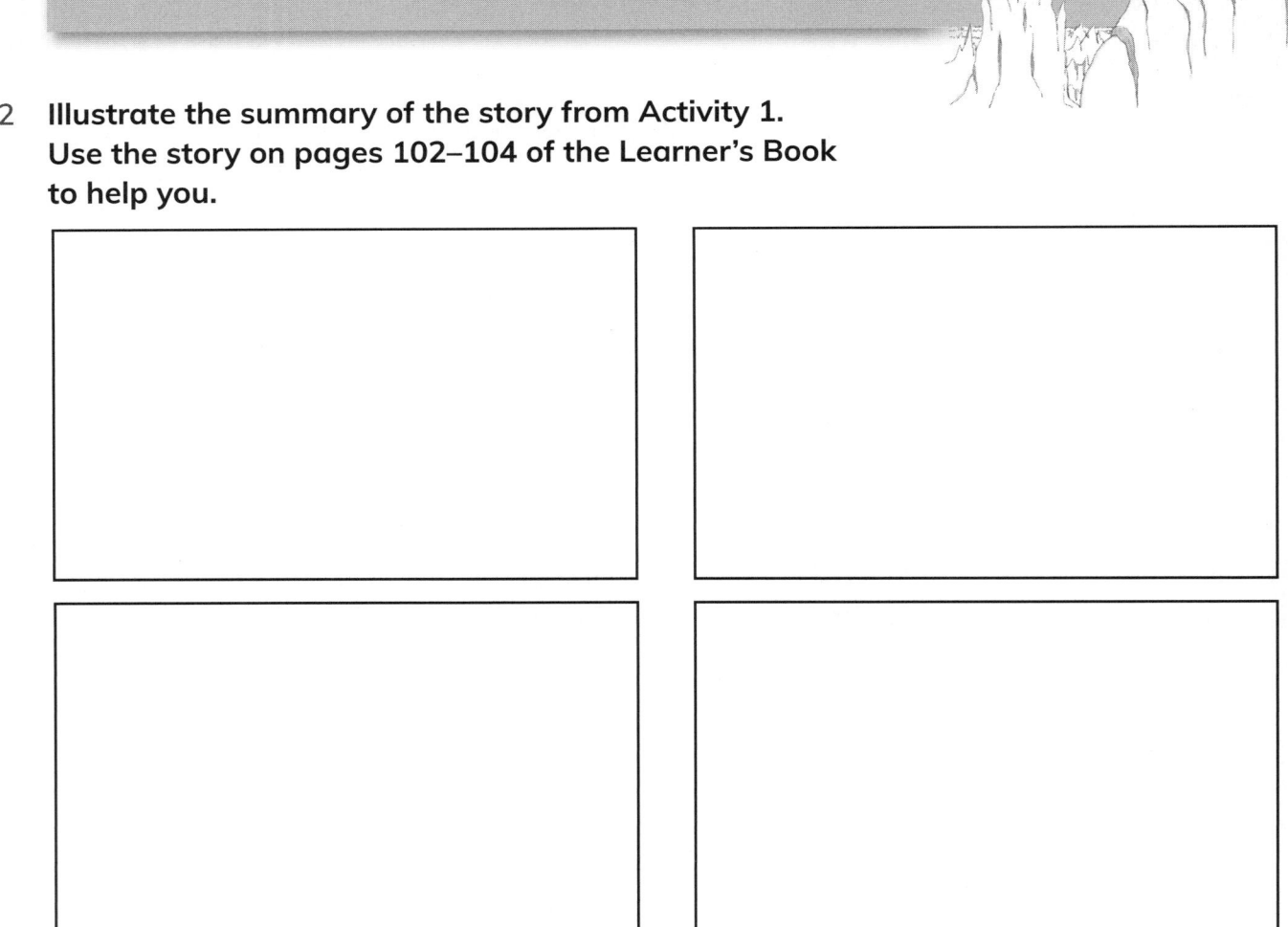

2   Illustrate the summary of the story from Activity 1.
    Use the story on pages 102–104 of the Learner's Book to help you.

6.5 Read and respond

3 Underline the similes in the sentences. Then match the similes to the pictures.

1 My brother eats like a horse, especially when he's been running.

2 That book must have been sad. Dad is crying like a baby.

3 Mia is a brilliant runner. She runs like the wind.

4 These jeans are great. They fit like a glove.

5 This rain is awful. It cuts like a knife.

a

b

c

d

e

4 Complete these sentences with these words from the story.

| politely | homesick | solve | hampered | echo | resumed |

a The mathematician can _____ problems without any difficulty.

b 'Can I help you?' asked the flower _____.

c The bad weather yesterday _____ the cyclists on their bike ride.

d The teacher _____ the class after break time.

e He felt _____ because he was away from his family and friends.

f He could hear the _____ of his voice in the huge, empty room.

5 **Values:** Answer this question with your opinion.

What's special for you about where you live?

_____

6 Great stories

> 6.6 Check your progress

Complete the sentences with information from the Learner's Book. Complete the crossword.

Across →

2 _____ painting is a popular form of Aboriginal art.

3 The outer part of a tree.

6 A story book with no words.

8 It cuts like a _____.

Down ↓

1 People who _____ talk about other people a lot.

3 She had a headache _____ she went to school.

4 Stories with a moral.

5 You feel _____ when you are unhappy because you are not at home for a long time.

7 I was _____ the newspaper when I heard a noise.

> 6.7 Reflection

Think about what you have studied in this unit. Answer the questions.

1   Which topics did you like and why?

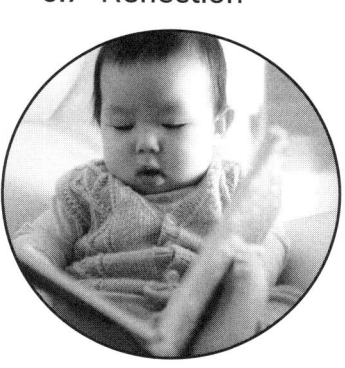

_____

_____

2   Which activities did you like and why?

_____

_____

3   What did you find challenging and why?

_____

_____

4   What help do you need now?

_____

_____

5   What do you want to find out more about?

_____

_____

7 Ancient Rome and Egypt

> 7.1 Why were these civilisations important?

1 **Vocabulary:** Match the words to the pictures.

> pyramids   sphinx   aqueduct
> canopic jar   gladiator   Roman numerals
> colosseum   mummy   Roman baths

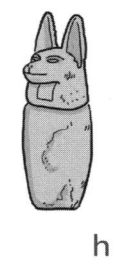

a
b
c
d
e
f
g
h
i

2 Complete the sentences about ancient civilisations with words from Activity 1.

a The ___pyramids___ were the tombs of the Egyptian pharaohs.
b A _____ fought against wild animals.
c People bathed in _____.
d All the organs (except the heart) of the dead pharaoh were put in a _____.
e Romans watched shows in a _____.
f A preserved body is called a _____.
g An _____ transported fresh water to the Roman city.
h The _____ guarded the tomb of the pharaoh.
i Romans used _____ to write numbers.

3 Look at these Egyptian hieroglyphic symbols. Can you translate this sentence?

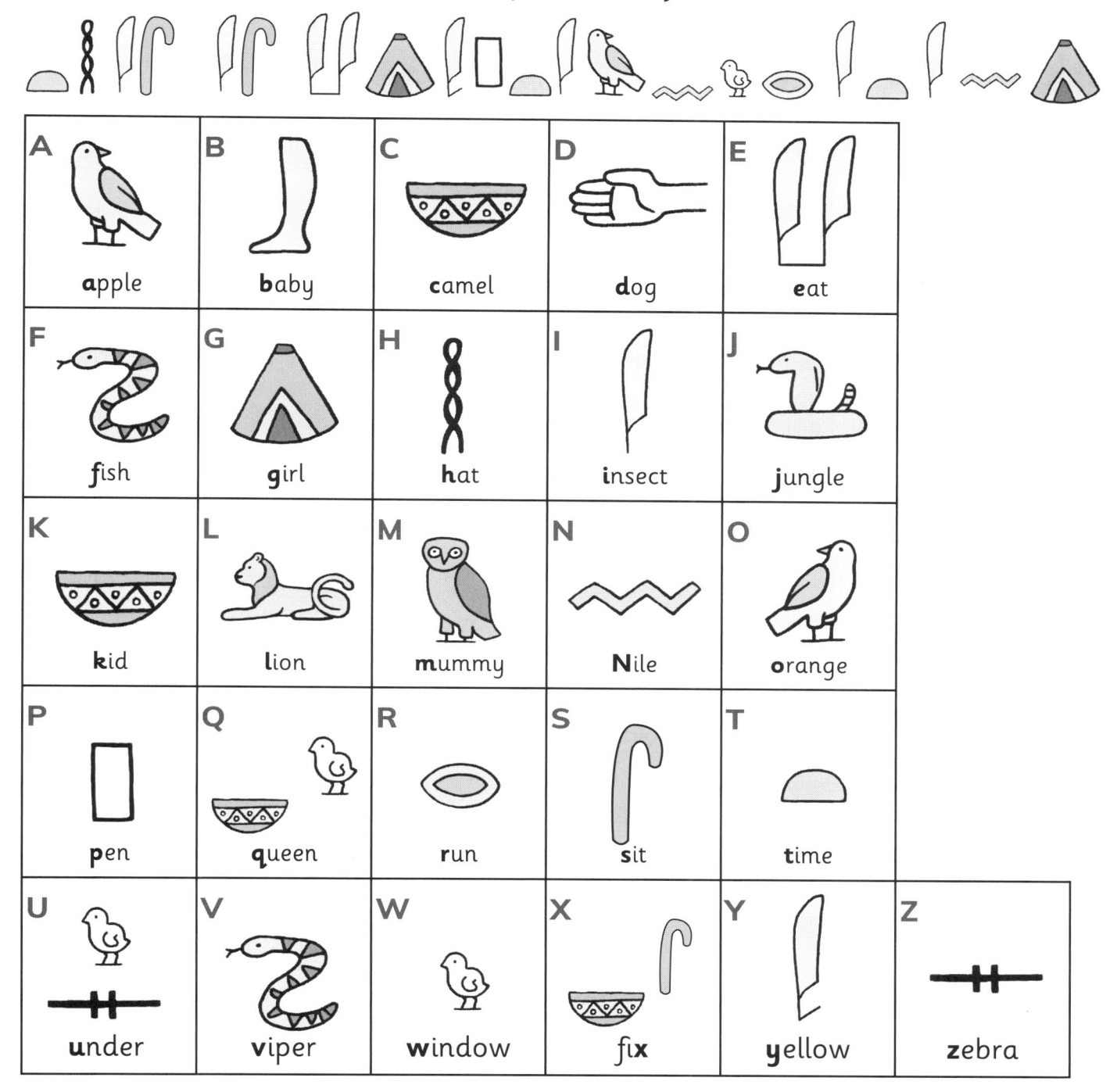

A apple	B baby	C camel	D dog	E eat
F fish	G girl	H hat	I insect	J jungle
K kid	L lion	M mummy	N Nile	O orange
P pen	Q queen	R run	S sit	T time
U under	V viper	W window	X fix	Y yellow	Z zebra

Challenge ⭐

4 Write words in your notebook using hieroglyphs for your partner to guess.

7 Ancient Rome and Egypt

> 7.2 Expressing opinions using *think, know, believe*

Use of English

We use the verbs **think, know** and **believe** to express opinions and beliefs.

I know that the name for an Egyptian king was pharaoh.
I think that aqueducts transported fresh water to Roman cities.
People believed that the Sphinx guarded the Pharaoh's tomb.

Focus

1 Complete these sentences with your opinion. Use 'I think / believe' or 'I don't think / believe.'

a I _____ the mummy was put in a sarcophagus.
b I _____ thieves robbed the pyramids of their treasures.
c I _____ a colosseum was similar in shape to a football stadium.
d I _____ hieroglyphics were a good way of communicating.
e I _____ people went to a colosseum for entertainment.

7.2 Use of English

Practice

2 Read Maya's description about the pyramids. Complete the sentences.

> **Get it right!**
>
> Remember, **don't use a comma!**
>
> ~~I think, that Romans wore togas.~~ ✗
>
> I think that Romans wore togas. ✓

The pyramids are amazing buildings! They were built as royal tombs of the kings in ancient Egypt. Archaeologists say that it took about 100,000 men about 20 years to build the Great Pyramid of Giza. Inside the pyramid there are secret passageways, rooms for all the pharaoh's and lots and lots of jewels and treasure. Some had trapdoors too, to catch robbers. I'm sure that the burial chambers were spectacular, and the beautiful paintings of the pharaoh's life must be very interesting to see. I'd love to visit the pyramids one day.

a Maya thinks <u>that the pyramids are amazing.</u>
b She knows that _____.
c Archaeologists know _____.
d Maya believes that _____.
e She knows that _____.

Challenge ⭐

3 Write a survey to discover your classmates' knowledge and opinions about ancient civilisations. Write your questions here.

a <u>Do you think that there are secret passageways in the pyramids? Why / Why not?</u>
b _____
c _____
d _____
e _____

7 Ancient Rome and Egypt

> 7.3 Imperative forms

Use of English

To form the imperative, we use the base form of the verb with no subject.

We use imperatives to:

- give orders
  Don't run in the corridor.

- give instructions
  Put your book in the drawer.

- give advice or warnings.
  Don't touch that – it's hot.

We can use 'please' to be more polite.
Please don't make so much noise.

Focus

1 **Put the words in order to make imperative sentences.**

   a shoes / Put / on / your / please.

   <u>Put your shoes on, please.</u>

   b late / Don't / school / be / for

   _____

   c mess / Don't / a / make

   _____

   d pyramid / Draw / for / a / please / tomorrow

   _____

   e Please / shout / don't / class/ in

   _____

   f more / Tutankhamen / about / Find / for / out / please / tomorrow

   _____

7.3 Use of English

Practice

2 Read the sentences about how mummies were made. Complete the instructions with the correct imperative.

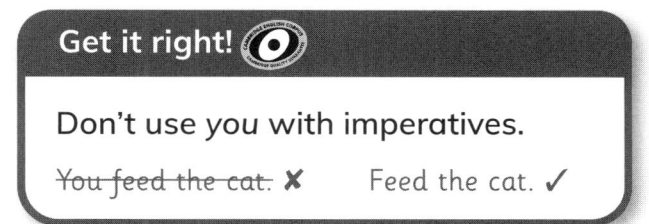

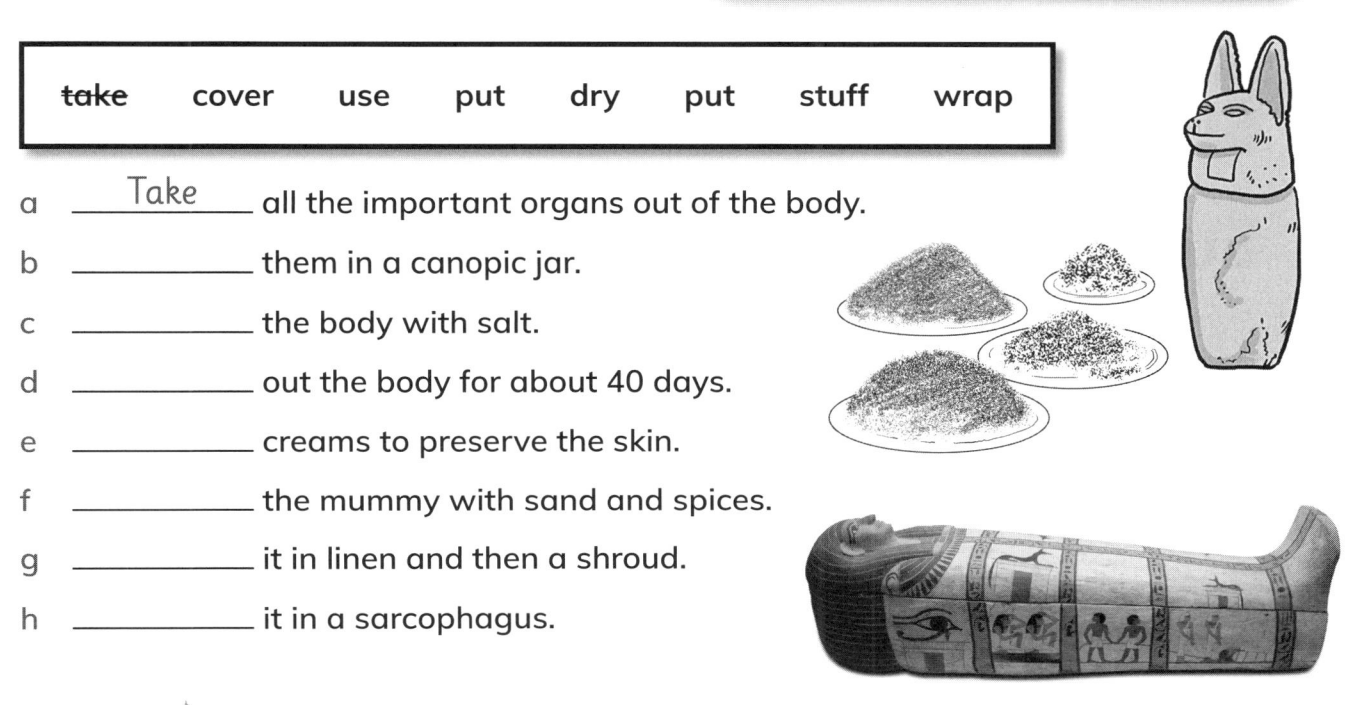

Get it right!

Don't use you with imperatives.

~~You feed the cat.~~ ✗   Feed the cat. ✓

| ~~take~~ | cover | use | put | dry | put | stuff | wrap |

a _____Take_____ all the important organs out of the body.
b _____ them in a canopic jar.
c _____ the body with salt.
d _____ out the body for about 40 days.
e _____ creams to preserve the skin.
f _____ the mummy with sand and spices.
g _____ it in linen and then a shroud.
h _____ it in a sarcophagus.

Challenge ⭐

3 Choose one of these places.
Write advice and rules for visitors using the imperative form.

| swimming pool | museum | cinema | wildlife sanctuary |

_____
_____
_____
_____

85

7 Ancient Rome and Egypt

> 7.4 An amazing discovery!

1 Read the article about the discovery of some surprising Roman artefacts in London. In your opinion, what was the most surprising discovery?

DAILY NEWS

Surprising discovery in London well

Yesterday, archaeologists discovered thousands of Roman artefacts at a building site in Central London. They discovered objects such as plates and bowls that Roman families ate their food on 2,000 years ago. 'They are in excellent condition,' said the archaeologist at the site. Historians believe that London was under attack at this time from Scotland and Germany, and the Romans left London in 410 CE. 'They were found at the bottom of a deep well, where they were probably put as the Romans left the city.'

The archaeologists discovered some even more surprising things!
There was an entire roman street, and the skull of a bear, which probably entertained the Romans at the nearby amphitheatre. Lots of Roman coins were found too. 'This is the best find in years!' said the archaeologist who discovered the well.

The well with some of the plates

More stories inside

2 Find examples in the text of the following.

a a quotation _____

b a fact _____

c an opinion _____

d a headline _____

7.4 Write about it

3 **Complete this summary about the discovery.**

The artefacts were found ¹<u>yesterday</u>. They were discovered by ²_____. The site was located at ³_____. Many objects and places were found such as: ⁴_____.

4 **Can you find an example of a preposition of time, position and location in the article?**

Prepositions	
Time:	in 410 CE
Location:	
Position:	

Language focus

Prepositions of time, location and position

Yesterday, **on** 24th November 1922 ...
(time)

... **in** the Valley of the Kings.
(location)

Challenge ⭐

5 Imagine you live in the future. You have discovered a time capsule full of everyday objects you use now. Write an article about what you have discovered.

- First think of and draw typical everyday items you use in the time capsule.
- Write the place and the year on the capsule.
- Write a headline.
- Write about the discovery: When, where, what, who.
- Include facts and opinions.

Place:
Year:

87

7 Ancient Rome and Egypt

> 7.5 Horatius at the Bridge

1. Imagine you are a Roman warrior living in the ancient city of Rome. Draw in your own notebook a picture of yourself wearing clothes and footwear from this time. Use the story on pages 120–123 of the Learner's Book to help you.

2. Now write a description about yourself. What is your Roman name? Include information about: clothes, housing, diet and your daily life.

_____
_____
_____
_____
_____

3. Read the story about *Horatius on the Bridge* again. Circle (T) or False (F).

    a The king of the Etruscans marched towards Rome with a small army of men.   T/F

    b The Romans thought they had enough men to fight them.   T/F

    c The people stayed inside the city while guards watched the roads.   T/F

    d The white-haired Fathers didn't know what to do.   T/F

    e A guard called Horatius cut down the bridge.   T/F

    f The bridge fell into the water making a great splash.   T/F

    g Horatius was hit by a spear thrown by one of Porsena's soldiers.   T/F

    h Horatius was the best swimmer in Rome, but he didn't reach the other side of the river.   T/F

7.5 Read and respond

4 Label the pictures with the words.

| spear | grateful | axe | leaped | swift |

a _____

b _____

c _____

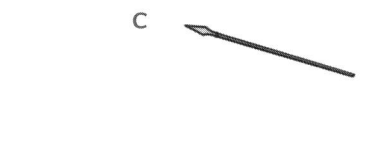

d _____

e _____

5 Complete these sentences with words from Activity 4.

  a He cut the tree down with an _____.

  b The elderly man was very _____ to the young girl who helped him cross the road.

  c The boy _____ across the big puddle.

  d She is a _____ runner.

  e He threw the _____, but missed his target.

Challenge

6 **Values: Being selfless**

  a How do you think about other people before yourself?
  Write a list of the things you do for other people.

  _____
  _____

  b Could you do more things to help other people?
  Make a resolution and write two of your intentions here.

  _____
  _____

89

7 Ancient Rome and Egypt

> 7.6 Check your progress

Choose the correct answers and write in the space.

1. The tombs were full of _____.
   a robbers
   b sand
   c jewels and treasures

2. _____ fought against wild animals in Ancient Rome.
   a soldiers
   b gladiators
   c merchants

3. Egyptian scribes wrote on _____.
   a reeds
   b papyrus paper
   c rice paper

4. They _____ the Pharaoh's body in salt.
   a stuffed
   b covered
   c wrapped

5. Creams were used to preserve the _____.
   a salt
   b skin
   c hair

6. Aqueducts transported _____ to Roman cities.
   a food
   b people
   c fresh water

7. _____ papyrus reed to make paper.
   a using
   b used
   c use

8. The year is _____ (MMXXI).
   a 2020
   b 2021
   c 2022

9. He discovered Roman artefacts _____ the bottom of a well in London.
   a at
   b on
   c in

10. Porsena's men _____ towards Horatius and the guards.
    a swift
    b dashed
    c fought

11. The guards used their _____ to cut down the bridge.
    a spears
    b hands
    c axes

> 7.7 Reflection

Think about what you have studied in this unit. Answer the questions.

1   Which topics did you like and why?

   _____

   _____

2   Which activities did you like and why?

   _____

   _____

3   What did you find challenging and why?

   _____

   _____

4   What help do you need now?

   _____

   _____

5   What do you want to find out more about?

   _____

   _____

8 Rainforests

> 8.1 What do you know about rainforests?

1 Read about the different parts of the rainforest and the animals which live there. Number the animals in the picture.

Emergent layer (A): This is the tallest layer in the forest, where there are giant trees Only fliers and gliders live here, such as the **harpy eagle (1)** and the **pygmy glider (2)**.

Canopy (B): This is the upper part of the leafy trees. It is full of animal life and the noisiest part of the forest. This is where the **sloth (3)** lives, as well as the **spider monkey (4)** and the **toucan (5)**.

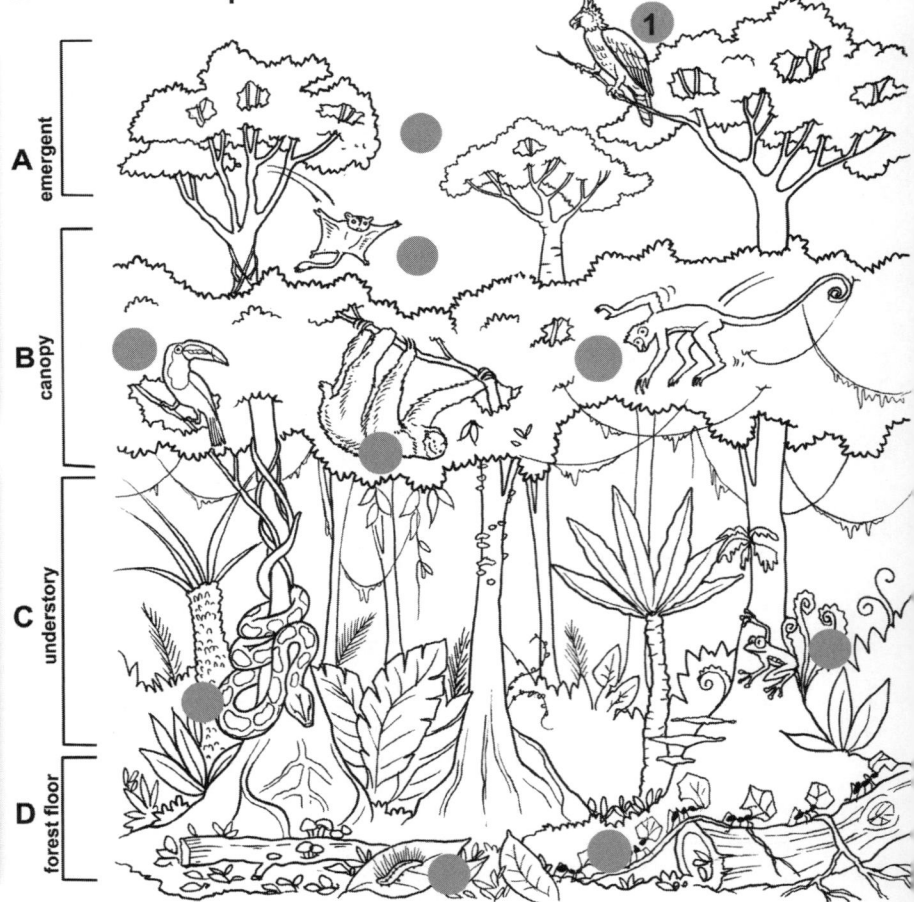

Understory (C): This is a cool, dark environment under the leaves of the trees. It is home to animals such as the **red-eyed tree frog (6)** and the **boa constrictor (7)**.

Forest floor (D): Many insects and other tiny creatures live here, such as the large **leafcutter ants (8)** and hairy **caterpillars (9)** with stinging hairs that protect them from predators.

8.1 Think about it

2   Read the text again and find:
    a   two insects _____ _____
    b   two superlative adjectives, one to describe the emergent layer and another the canopy _____ _____
    c   two birds _____ _____
    d   two adjectives to describe the understory _____ _____
    e   another word for *insects* _____
    f   an amphibian _____

3   How do rainforests protect the world's climate?
    Study and label the picture with these words.

    | carbon dioxide | oxygen | greenhouse gas | natural resources |

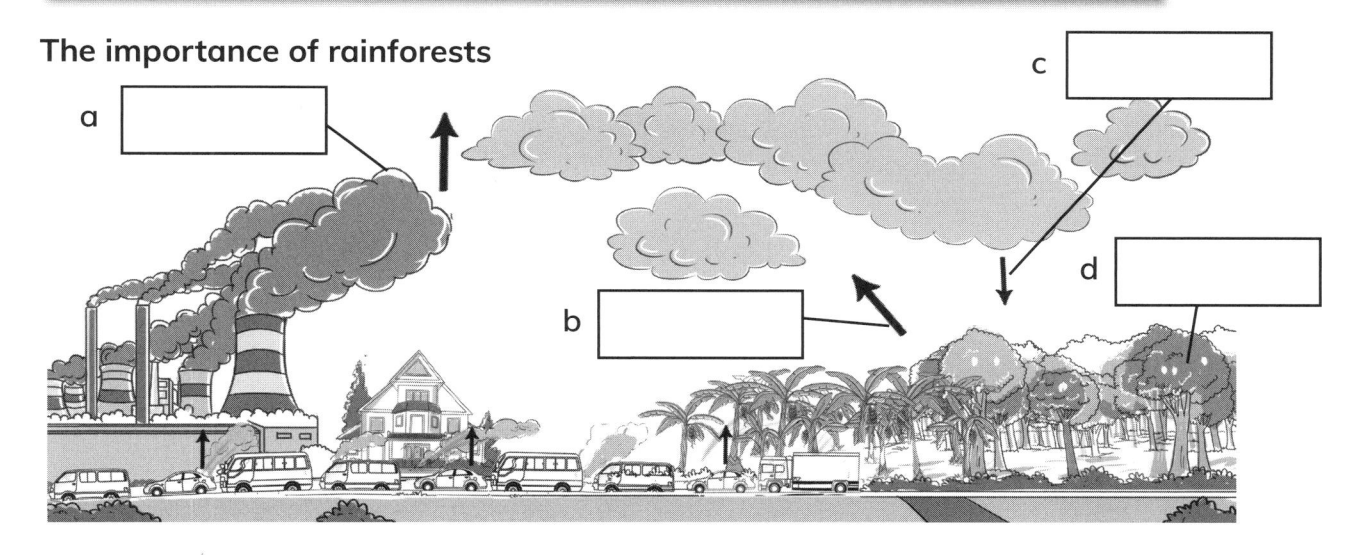

    The importance of rainforests

    a ____
    b ____
    c ____
    d ____

Challenge ⭐

4   Write sentences describing what you can see in the picture.
    The picture shows how rainforests protect our climate. Carbon dioxide …
    _____
    _____
    _____

8 Rainforests

> 8.2 The present perfect

Use of English

We use the present perfect when we are talking about experiences up to the present.

We use **for** and **since** with the present perfect to say how long something has been true. We use **for** with periods of time and **since** for the starting point in the past.

for	since
10 minutes	8 o'clock
five days	Monday
three years	yesterday
a century	2018

They've lived in the forest
for hundreds of years. (period of time)
They've lived in the forest
since the 1800s. (starting point)

Focus

1 Complete the sentences using the present perfect. Circle for or since.

The Yanomami tribe ¹_____ (live) in the rainforest ²**since / for** centuries, and they ³_____ (hunt) the land ⁴**since / for** the 1800s. But their way of life ⁵_____ (be) in danger ⁶**since / for** years. Deforestation ⁷_____ (be) a serious problem ⁸**since / for** 70 years, and they ⁹_____ (have) less land to hunt on ¹⁰**since / for** men started cutting down the rainforest.

8.2 Use of English

Practice

2 Write these time expressions in the correct column.

> 2011   three days   last Friday
> five hours   March   four years

Get it right!

Remember to use the correct tense.

~~I didn't see her since last week.~~ ✗

I haven't seen her since last week. ✓

For: _____, _____, _____

Since: _____, _____, _____

3 Write sentences using the present perfect. Use *for* or *since*.

a I / live / my house / nine years
<u>I have lived in my house for nine years.</u>

b He / not be / at my school / long
_____.

c We / live / in this town / I was born
_____.

d I / know / my best friend / 2016
_____.

e She / be / in Tokyo / March
_____.

Challenge ⭐

4 Write sentences about your experiences. Write three affirmative sentences and three negative sentences. You can use these verbs in the present perfect or ones of your own.

> play   study   do   have   be   travel   meet

<u>I've been to Thailand with my family. I haven't travelled on a plane.</u>

8 Rainforests

> 8.3 Adverbs of degree

Use of English

Adverbs of degree are used to show the intensity or degree of something. They can be used before adjectives, verbs or other adverbs.

Before an adjective

Life is **very** difficult for tribes living in the rainforest.

It's **rather** cold today.

It's **extremely** hot today!

Before another adverb

I ate **quite** quickly.

We get on **fairly** well.

She looked a **little** better.

Before a verb

I **really** like your shirt.

Focus

1 Circle the best adverb in each sentence. Look at the whole sentence.

 a My homework was **a little / very** difficult. I couldn't do it.

 b It's **really / quite** hot today, so don't forget your sun cream.

 c Some of my friends are **a little / extremely** good at maths, but I find it hard.

 d I can't understand her at all because she speaks **quite / really** fast.

 e I **quite / fairly** like watching films on the TV, but I prefer going to the cinema.

8.3 Use of English

Practice

2 Read the text and complete it with the phrases from the box.

Rainforest facts!

- The Amazon rainforest in South America is
  ¹ _extremely big_. It covers over five and a half a
  million square kilometres. That's ² _____
  for just one rainforest. If it were a country, it would be
  the ninth biggest in the world.

- It's ³ _____ and dark in the understory. In fact, only two percent
  of the sunlight there reaches through the canopy of trees above.

- Rain can take a ⁴ _____ to travel from a rainforest's thick
  canopy to the floor – it can take ten minutes!

- The Korowai people of New Guinea live in houses that are ⁵ _____.
  Their tree houses are as high as 45m off the ground!

- Rainforest plants are ⁶ _____. Did you know that a quarter
  of the ingredients in modern medicines come from rainforests?

quite a large area	a little unusual
really important	fairly long time
~~extremely big~~	rather cool

Get it right!

Watch out for spelling errors!

It's ~~quiet~~ **quite** an interesting book.

Challenge ⭐

3 Find five more fun facts about the rainforest.
  How many adverbs of degree can you use?

_____
_____
_____
_____

8 Rainforests

> 8.4 Rainforest animals

1 What am I? Read the descriptions of the rainforest animals and match them to the correct picture.

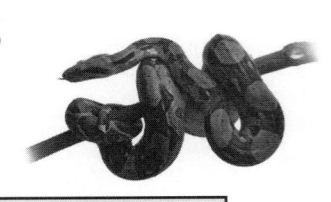

b boa constrictor
a harpy eagle 
c pygmy glider 
d toucan 

1 This animal lives in the canopy of the rainforest. It's mainly a fruit-eater, although it sometimes likes to catch a lizard or snake from the forest floor. It's got a big yellow and brown sharp bill (similar to a beak) that it uses to pick and throw fruit. __

2 This little animal lives in the giant trees and the canopy of the rainforest. It eats insects and fruit as well as pollen. It is about the size of a mouse. It has a brown, black and white tummy and a very long, thin, feathery tail. __

3 This long animal lives in the understory of the rainforest. It is a great hunter and likes to surprise its prey. It eats birds, frogs, lizards and rodents. It is very strong and it has circular and oval-shaped brown patterns on its body. __

4 This animal lives in the emergent trees of the rainforest. It has a pale, grey head, black outer feathers and white under feathers. It likes to eat monkeys and sloths. __

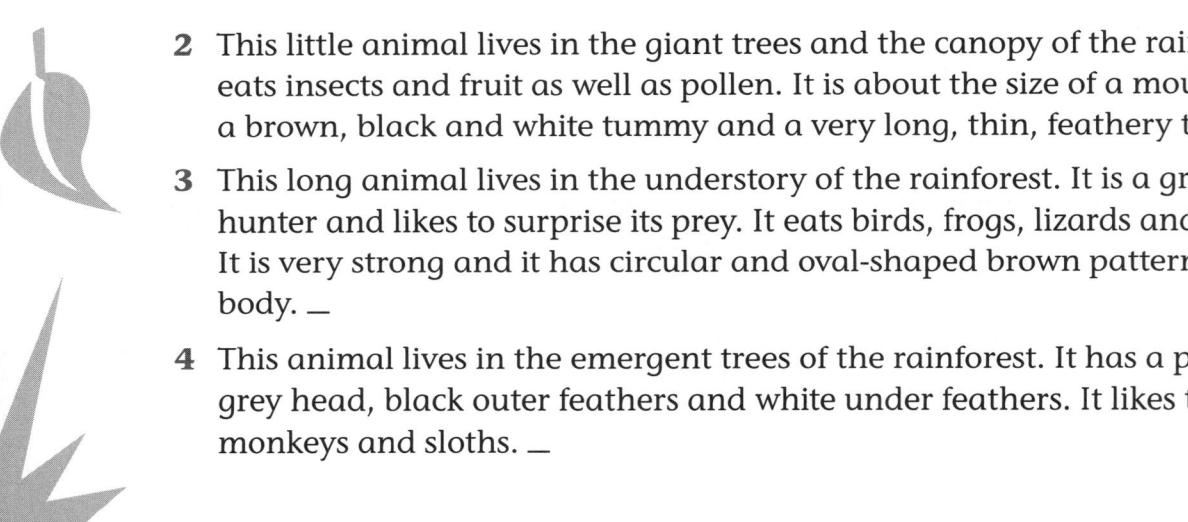

2 Read the sentences and circle true (T) or false (F).

a A toucan eats fruit, lizards and snakes. T / F
b A pygmy glider is bigger than a mouse. T / F
c A pygmy glider lives in the emergent layer. T / F
d A boa constrictor is an extremely good hunter. T / F
e A harpy eagle has white outer feathers and black under feathers. T / F

8.4 Write about it

> **Language focus**
>
> **Adjective order**
>
> When we use more than one adjective to describe a noun, the adjectives need to be in the following order:
>
> | 1 | 2 | 3 | 4 | 5 | 6 | 7 | 8 | 9 |
> |---|---|---|---|---|---|---|---|---|
> | Number → | Opinion → | Size → | Shape → | Age → | Colour → | Origin → | Material → | Noun |
> | Three | fabulous | big | fat | old | brown | Costa Rican | furry | sloths |

3 Reorder the adjectives to make sentences about the animals.

 a amazing / long / thin/ An / tail / feathery
    An amazing long, thin, feathery tail.

 b tree frog / Brazilian / A / green / small
    _____

 c African / large / beautiful / grey / parrot / A
    _____

 d frightening / brown / Two / crocodiles / long-bodied / Australian
    _____

 e Three / orangutans / enormous / long-haired
    _____

Challenge ⭐

4 In your notebook, write a description about the animal in the picture. Use the information in the fact file to help you.

Fact File

Location: rainforests of Central and South America.

Appearance: light brown or orange with black spots, sharp claws and teeth

Diet: fish, turtles, deer, tapirs

Behaviour: loves water, a good swimmer, sometimes climbs trees

a jaguar

8.5 A visit with Mr Tree Frog and *If I were a sloth*

1 **Read** the poem *A visit with Mr Tree Frog* again and find the following:
   a An adjective which describes his size. ____tiny____ (verse 1)
   b Another word for friend. _____ (verse 1)
   c A noise he makes. _____ (verse 2)
   d What his toes do at night. _____ (verse 3)
   e Something he likes to eat. _____ (verse 4)
   f Something he likes to eat on special occasions. _____ (verse 4)
   g Something he's famous for. _____ (verse 6)
   h Something his eyes do. _____ (verse 7)
   i Something he likes to do during the day. _____ (verse 7)
   j A superlative adjective. _____ (verse 8)

2 **Read** the sentences and circle true (T) or false (F). Correct the false sentences in your notebook.
   a Mr Tree Frog is very green. T / F
   b He likes danger and often fights. T / F
   c His slime can make you better. T / F
   d He closes his eyes when he is resting. T / F
   e He likes to play during the day. T / F

3 **Pronunciation:** Match the rhyming words.

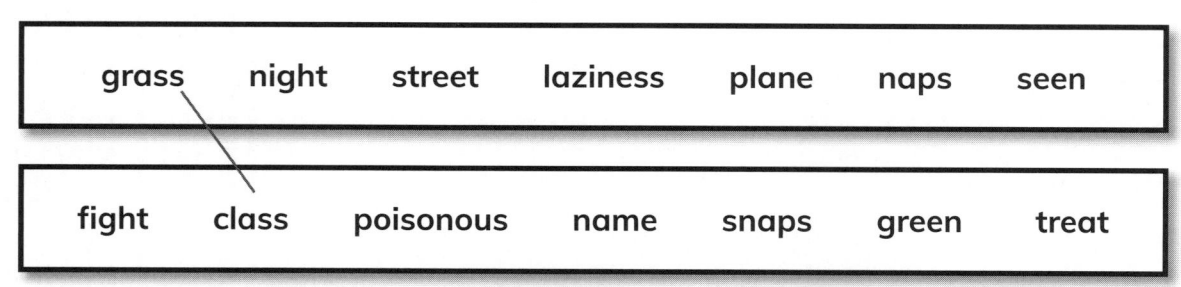

| grass | night | street | laziness | plane | naps | seen |

| fight | class | poisonous | name | snaps | green | treat |

8.5 Read and respond

4 Read the poem *If I were a sloth* again and (circle) the correct answer in the sentences below.

   a The sloth **sits in the trees / hangs upside down**.

   b The sloth sleeps all day in the **understory / canopy of the rainforest**.

   c It plays when the sun **comes up / goes down**.

   d It eats **at night / during the day**.

   e It **doesn't like the noise of birds / makes a similar noise to a bird**.

   f It is **a common / an endangered** animal in the rainforest.

   g It has **long / extremely long** arms.

   h People will **look at me in interest / not see me**.

Challenge ⭐

5 Write similes about the tree frog.

   a The frog is green like the grass.

   b It's busy _____.

   c It eats _____.

6 **Values:** How can we protect the tree frog's habitat? Write sentences with your ideas.

   a We can _____

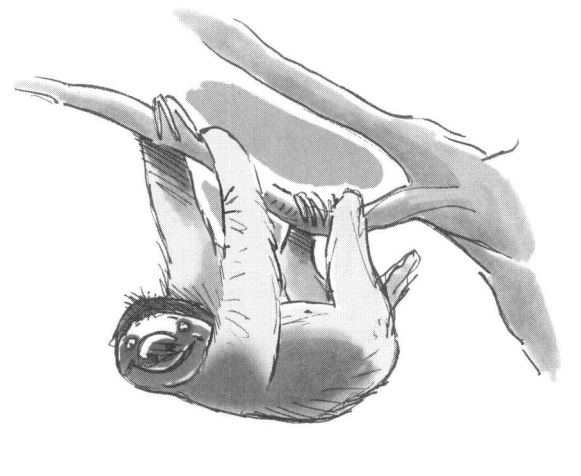

   b _____

   c _____

8 Rainforests

> 8.6 Check your progress

1 **Vocabulary:** Complete the sentences with a word from the box.

| forest floor | understory | oxygen | emergent layer | carbon dioxide |

a The top part of the rainforest is called the _____.
b _____ is a greenhouse gas.
c Rainforests take carbon dioxide from the air and release _____ for us to breathe in.
d The _____ is underneath the canopy.
e The _____ is very quiet and has very little sunlight.

2 **Use of English:** Circle the correct answer.

Have you ever [1] **went / been** to a rainforest? Well, if you [2] **hasn't / haven't** been to one before, be prepared for [3] **a little / very** hot weather. The rainforests are near the equator and are [4] **extremely / a little** wet and humid too.

When you take a trip into the forest, you will see many of the wonderful animals and insects that live there. You might see the toucan with its [5] **big, sharp / sharp, big** bill, or the harpy eagle with its [6] **feathery, pale / grey, feathery** head. The [7] **brown, old, fat / fat, old, brown** sloth could be hugging a tree and if you listen carefully you might hear the rattle of the [8] **green, tiny / tiny, green** red-eyed tree frog.

Challenge ⭐

3 Find out about another rainforest animal.
Write sentences in your notebook about its appearance, its diet and behaviour.

> 8.7 Reflection

Think about what you have studied in this unit. Answer the questions.

1 Which topics did you like and why?

   _____

   _____

2 Which activities did you like and why?

   _____

   _____

3 What did you find challenging and why?

   _____

   _____

4 What help do you need now?

   _____

   _____

5 What do you want to find out more about?

   _____

   _____

9 Animal kingdom

> 9.1 Animal habitats

1 Do the animal quiz.

a Which reptile lives in the Sahara Desert in Africa? _____

b Which fish is very colourful and lives in the Indian and Pacific oceans? _____

c Which amphibian is very tiny and lives in African rivers? _____

d What does a stick insect eat? _____

e Why is the clownfish's habitat in danger? _____

f Where does the elephant seal live? _____

g What is the elephant seal's diet? _____

h Which bird of prey lives in the Swiss mountains? _____

i What is a hare? _____

j What does an antelope have to protect itself? _____

9.1 Think about it

2 Read this short text about the Orca and underline information about:

   a its characteristics   c its diet
   b its habitat   d a surprising fact.

> Orcas live in the world's oceans. They are enormous mammals that can grow to 9–10 metres in length. Their backs are black and their stomachs are white, which means their prey might not see them and don't notice that they are in danger. They can eat up to 227 kilograms of food each day! Together in groups they hunt warm-blooded animals such as seals, sea lions and sea turtles.

3 Circle three preposition + noun examples in the text.

4 Warm-blooded is a compound noun.
   Can you find two more compound nouns in the text?

   _____   _____

5 Now write a short text about zebras using information from the fact file.
   Use Activity 2 to help you.

Fact File

Habitat: savannah, Africa. They move in herds of 10–15.

Characteristics: From the Equidae family, black and white stripes.

Diet: Grass.

Curious fact: Stands up while sleeping.

9 Animal kingdom

> 9.2 It / Its

> **Use of English**
>
> We use **it** to give further information about a topic that we have already talked about. This is so that we don't repeat the name again.
>
> The chameleon is a reptile. **It** has got scales.
> ↑
> the chameleon
>
> **Its** is the possessive form of **it**. We use **its** if something belongs to the person or animal.
>
> It changes **its** colour to protect itself from predators.

Focus

1 Read and circle *it* or *its* in each sentence.

a The African elephant is the largest animal walking the Earth. **(It)** / **Its** has got a long trunk.

b A monkey uses **it** / **its** long tail to help swing from tree to tree.

c The clownfish is in danger because **it** / **its** habitat is dying.

d The giraffe needs **it** / **its** long neck to reach the high leaves on the trees during a drought.

e The kangaroo is native to Australia. **It** / **Its** has got two strong back legs for jumping.

f My cat is very clever. **It** / **Its** can find **it** / **its** food even if I hide it!

9.2 Use of English

> **Get it right!**
>
> Remember to use the personal pronoun *it* and the possessive pronoun *its* correctly.
>
> ~~It's camouflage protects it from predators.~~ ✗
>
> *Its* camouflage protects it from predators. ✓

Practice

2   Complete the sentences with *it* or *its*.

   a   The zebra lives on the savannah. ____It____ has got black and white stripes. _____ stripes protect _____ from predators.

   b   The kangaroo lives in herds in Australia. _____ uses _____ powerful legs to kick predators.

   c   The giraffe is the tallest living land animal. _____ long neck helps _____ to reach the high leaves on the trees.

   d   When an elephant is hot, _____ flaps _____ large ears to help _____ cool down.

   e   The male antelope has horns. _____ uses _____ horns to protect itself from predators.

Challenge ⭐

3   Can you make sentences about these animals? Use *it* and *its*. Use the prompts to help you.

   a   The cuttlefish is also known as the ink fish. ink / protect from predators.
       Its ink protects it from predators.

   b   The camel lives in dry countries. two humps / store fat / give energy.
       _____

   c   The chameleon is a lizard. changes skin colour / protect from predators
       _____

9 Animal kingdom

> 9.3 Gerunds and infinitives

Use of English

We use the **gerund (-ing)** after some verbs, for example *enjoy, dislike, finish, keep, prefer, stop* and *practise*.

I **enjoy** spend**ing** time with my family.
I didn't enjoy spending time in the mountains.
I **prefer** skateboard**ing** to riding my bike.

After other verbs we use **to + infinitive**, for example *want, need, forget, study* and *hope*.

I **want to start** dance classes after school.
I **forgot to finish** my English homework last night.

Focus

1 Read and circle the correct form of the verb gerund or to + infinitive.

a She decided **going** / **to go** for a run in the countryside.
b I dislike **cleaning** / **to clean** my bedroom at the weekends.
c I keep to **sing** / **singing** that song. I love it!
d I hope **passing** / **to pass** my English test next week.
e I stopped **to play** / **playing** the violin when I was seven.
f I hope **visiting** / **to visit** my friend in Turkey next summer.

Get it right!

Don't forget **to**!

Keep a list in your notebook of verbs followed by the gerund and verbs with **to** + infinitive.

~~I need get up early tomorrow.~~ ✗
I need to get up early tomorrow. ✓

Practice

2 Read the news report about how a man helped an injured athlete.
Use the verbs in the box to complete the report. Use gerunds or to + infinitive.

| be   run   call   get up   take   stop |

Jamie enjoys ¹ _running_ in the mountains at the weekend. Yesterday he wanted ² _____ a more difficult route because it was a lovely sunny day. He kept ³ _____ to look at the spectacular views of the city below.

Then, he came across some very rocky ground. He had ⁴ _____ careful so he didn't fall over, but his foot got stuck. He fell and hurt his ankle. He needed ⁵ _____ but he couldn't walk. He decided ⁶ _____ the police, but he had no battery on his phone. Luckily, a man was walking his dog and came to his rescue.

Challenge ★

3 Can you complete the captions for these pictures?
Remember to use either a gerund or infinitive after the verb.

a Keep _____!

b Remember _____.

c Stop _____!

9 Animal kingdom

> 9.4 Animal rescue

1 Complete the dialogue below with information from the leaflet.

The WILD ANIMAL Sanctuary

Species: emus, bears, African lions, tigers, foxes, raccoons, lynx ... and more!

Days: Sunday to Saturday (Mondays closed)

Opening times: 9 a.m. to 8 p.m.

Price: Adults: $10 **Adults over 65 years:** $7.50
Children (3–12 years): $7
Children under 2 years: free admission

SPECIAL SUMMER EVENTS
Summer Safari and Fair Saturday 12th July
Summer Concert 'Wild Rock!' Friday 18th July

Mum: Look at this leaflet about the Wild Animal Sanctuary, Adam. Do you want to go there in the school holidays?

Adam: Yes – what can you see there?

Mum: There are lots of amazing animals to see! There are emus and bears, and wild cats too, like ¹_____, ²_____ and ³_____.

Adam: OK, that sounds great! What days is it open?

Mum: Hmmm ... It ⁴_____.

Adam: ... and what time does it open and close?

Mum: ⁵_____.

Adam: Right, so we can spend all day there! How much will two tickets cost?

Mum: ⁶_____.

Adam: Are there any special activities on?

Mum: Yes, there's a Summer safari and fair and a ⁷_____.

Adam: I love concerts! Let's go on ⁸_____ to visit the sanctuary.

9.4 Write about it

2 Problem solving: Work out how much it will cost these families to visit the Wild Animal Sanctuary.

a Ticket cost: $ _____

b Ticket cost: $ _____

c Ticket cost: $ _____

3 Design and write a leaflet for the Summer safari and fair at the Wild Animal Sanctuary.
- Use the model on page 150 in the Learner's Book to help you.
- Find out about the types of activities safari parks offer online, for example watching feeding time. Include some in your leaflet.
- Draw a picture of your favourite wild animal in your leaflet.

Summer safari and fair

Date: _____

Time: _____

Price: _____

Special activities:

_____

_____

_____

111

9 Animal kingdom

> 9.5 Mum won't let me keep a rabbit

1   **Read** the poem in the Learner's Book again and label the pictures with the correct names.

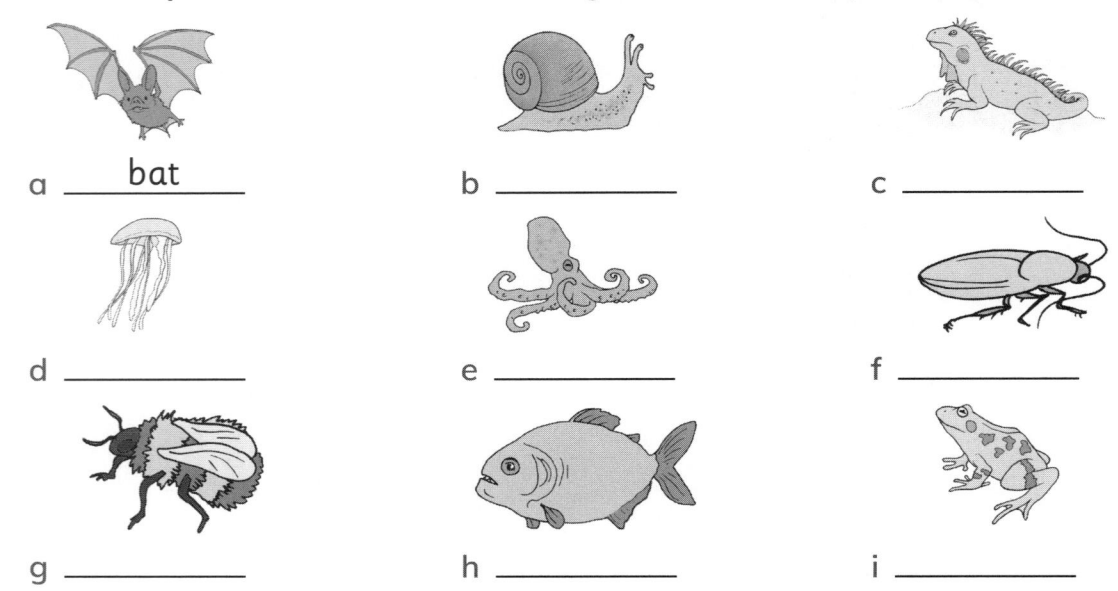

a ___bat___   b _____   c _____

d _____   e _____   f _____

g _____   h _____   i _____

2   **Vocabulary:** Find and circle the animals the child in the poem can't keep.

rabbitporcupinepigeonantwombatmambaelephantkangarooearwigwildebeest

3   **Pronunciation:** Complete the sentences with a rhyming word from the poem.

   a   The _____ flew over the **cat**.
   b   The **whale** said, 'Hello' to the _____.
   c   The **duck** was in _____.
   d   There was a _____ in the **tree**.
   e   The _____ had a **feast**.

   | flea | bat | luck |
   | wildebeest | snail | |

4   Circle the odd one out in each category and add one of your own.

   a   **Mammals**   porcupine   water-rat   ant   _____
   b   **Insects**   flea   duck   bumblebee   _____
   c   **Birds**   pigeon   mallard duck   toad   _____

112

9.5 Read and respond

5 Reorder the words to make an animal alliteration and match to the correct picture.

1   2   3   4

a   lazy / log / leopard / the / lies / Larry / the / lazily / on

_____.

b   Betty / busy / the / buzzes / busily / bumblebee

_____.

c   flies / Felicity / flea / the / fat / fabulously

_____.

d   slowly / slimy / Sid / slides / the / snail

_____.

6 Choose your favourite animal from the poem. Draw a picture of it.
  Find out and complete the information below.

My favourite animal is: _____

Type of animal: _____

Diet: _____

Habitat: _____

Characteristics: _____

7 **Values:** Choose an animal from this unit and explain what we can do to protect it.

_____

_____

_____

9 Animal kingdom

> 9.6 Check your progress

1 Complete the crossword.

Across →

3 A grassy habitat with few trees.

5 Another name for the killer whale.

8 An animal that hunts and kills other animals.

10 A chameleon can change _____ colour.

Down ↓

1 How animals protect themselves from predators.

2 The parrot enjoyed _____ breakfast with Hannah.

4 The insect the poet keeps in his garden.

6 A zebra has black and white ones.

7 An amphibian.

9 A very dry habitat.

Challenge ⭐

2 Make a revision crossword to test your friends!

> 9.7 Reflection

Think about what you have studied in this unit. Answer the questions.

1 Which topics did you like and why?

   _____
   _____

2 Which activities did you like and why?

   _____
   _____

3 What did you find challenging and why?

   _____
   _____

4 What help do you need now?

   _____
   _____

5 What do you want to find out more about?

   _____
   _____

Acknowledgements

The authors and publishers acknowledge the following sources of copyright material and are grateful for the permissions granted. While every effort has been made, it has not always been possible to identify the sources of all the material used, or to trace all copyright holders. If any omissions are brought to our notice, we will be happy to include the appropriate acknowledgements on reprinting.

Unit 1 'Our teacher's multi-talented' by Kenn Nesbitt, used with the permission of the author; 'Super Samson Simpson' from *Something Big Has Been Here* by Jack Prelutsky illustrated by James Stevenson. TEXT COPYRIGHT © 1990 BY JACK PRELUTSKY, ILLUSTRATIONS COPYRIGHT © 1990 BY JAMES STEVENSON Used by permission of HarperCollins Publishers; **Unit 3** 'The Lost City' by Margo Fallis, used and adapted with permission from the author; **Unit 4** Text and illustrations from *Horrid Henry's Birthday Party* by Francesca Simon, illustrations by Tony Ross, reproduced by permission of Orion Children's Books, an imprint of Hachette Children's Books, Carmelite House, 50 Victoria Embankment, London imprint, EC4Y 0DZ; **Unit 5** Extracts and illustrations from The Girl Who Thought in Pictures: The story of Dr Temple Grandin by Julia Finley Mosca, illustrations by Daniel Rieley, © 2017 The Innovation Press; **Unit 6** Excerpts from *The Little Prince* by Antoine De Saint-Exupery translated by Richard Howard, reprinted by permission of Houghton Mifflin Harcourt Publishing Company, illustrations and audio use © Editions Gallimard **Unit 7** 'Horatius at the Bridge' James Baldwin; **Unit 8** 'A visit with Mr. Tree Frog' and 'If I were a sloth' by Kathy Paysen from her *Rainbows in the Rainforest Collection*; **Unit 9** 'Mum Won't Let Me Keep a Rabbit' from *Gargling with Jelly* by Brian Patten (Viking, 1985) Copyright© Brian Patten, 1985 and Reproduced by permission of the author c/o Rogers, Coleridge & White Ltd., and Penguin Random House UK.

Thanks to the following for permission to reproduce images:

Cover by Pablo Gallego (Beehive Illustration); *Inside* Unit 1 Mohd Hafiez Mohd Razali/GI; Jose Luis Pelaez Inc/GI; Planet Flem/GI; calvindexter/GI; Kelvin Murray/GI; Alistair Berg/GI; Kelvin Murray/GI; Alistair Berg/GI; Manfred Gottschalk/GI; Mixetto/GI; Adie Bush/GI; Adie Bush/GI; Kali9/GI; Jose Luis Pelaez Inc/GI; Jose Luis Pelaez Inc/GI; Hraun/GI; Ian Thwaites/Alamy Stock Photo; PhotoAlto/Sigrid Olsson/GI; RichVintage/GI; PhotoAlto/Sigrid Olsson/GI; Katelyn Mulcahy/GI; Westend61/GI; Jim Cummins/GI; Sorrapong Apidech/GI; Richard Newstead/GI; Unit 2 krisanapong detraphiphat/GI; Westend61/GI; Mrs/GI; filadendron/GI; Blend Images-JGI/Jamie Grill/GI; Jose Luis Pelaez Inc/GI; Claudia Totir/GI; RapidEye/GI; Jose Luis Pelaez Inc/GI; Claudia Totir/GI; RapidEye/GI; Madmaxer/GI; Tito Atchaa/GI; Photo and Co/GI; South China Morning Post/GI; Clerkenwell/GI; Stuart Minzey/GI; Fuse/GI; Clerkenwell/GI; Stuart Minzey/GI; Fuse/GI; Lew Robertson/GI; Lew Robertson/GI; ROGER HARRIS/SCIENCE PHOTO LIBRARY/GI; Roger Harris/Science Photo Librar/GI; Unit 3 Landscapes, Seascapes, Jeweller & Action Photography/GI; Artur Debat/GI; Cavan Images/GI; Tanatat pongphibool ,thailand/GI; F.J. Jimenez/Gi; e55evu/GI; Xavier Arnau Serrat/GI; Image Source/GI; Getty Images/GI; GeorgePeters/GI; Image Source/GI; GeorgePeters/GI; MeijiShowa/

Alamy Stock Photo; TommL/GI; Enrico Calderoni/GI; Enrico Calderoni/GI; Everett Collection Inc/Alamy Stock Photo; NINA PROMMER/EPA-EFE/Shutterstock; PictureLux/The Hollywood Archive/Alamy Stock Photo; Thomas Winz/GI; Thomas Winz/GI; luxizeng/GI; Luxizeng/GI; Tanatat pongphibool,thailand/GI; e55evu/GI; Morsa Images/GI; aabejon/GI; Unit 4 ferrantraite/GI; South China Morning Post/GI; Tim Macpherson/GI; Roberto Soncin Gerometta/GI; Travel Ink/GI; Global_Pics/GI; Fuse/GI; ZUMA Press, Inc./Alamy Stock Photo; Getty Images/GI; DANIEL LEAL-OLIVAS/GI; Sergio Mendoza Hochmann/GI; SOPA Images/GI; Jeremy Woodhouse/GI; jane/GI; Westend61/GI; Asia Images Group/GI; Westend61/GI; Asia Images Group/GI; 500px Asia/GI; vinhdav/GI; Christine Müller/GI; Richard Hutchings/GI; Erika Eros/GI; Richard Hutchings/GI; Erika Eros/GI; DigiPub/GI; Ana Silva/GI; DigiPub/GI; Ana Silva/GI; Unit 5 Steve Russell/GI; Steve Russell/GI; Roberto Machado Noa/GI; JGI/GI; JGI/Tom Grill/GI; Image Source/GI; Image Source/GI; Ilyabolotov/GI; Aja Koska/GI; Dp_photo/GI; Dp_photo/GI; Unit 6 Rich Legg/GI; YASSER AL-ZAYYAT/GI; Fstop123/GI; Thomas Lai Yin Tang/GI; Universal History Archive/GI; Catherine Falls Commercial/GI; Catherine Falls Commercial/GI; Transcendental Graphics/GI; Frank Rothe/GI; Jordan Lye/GI; Westend61/GI; dedoma/Shutterstock; Peter Unger/GI; Peter Unger/GI; 130920/GI; Nattaya Mahaum/GI; Nattaya Mahaum/GI; Unit 7 Kenneth Alan Brown/GI; Miguel Sanz/GI; danbreckwoldt/GI; LianeM/GI; Harold M. Lambert/GI; x-drew/GI; Izzet Keribar/GI; FotografiaBasica/GI; Izzet Keribar/GI; FotografiaBasica/GI; Skaman306/GI; THEPALMER/GI; Fred Bahurlet/GI; Zhengjie Wu/GI; By Eve Livese/GI; Alexander Spatari/GI; Duncan1890/GI; Skaman306/GI; THEPALMER/GI; Fred Bahurlet/GI; By Eve Livesey/GI; Duncan1890/GI; LianeM/GI; ChiccoDodiFC/GI; Grant Faint/GI; Harold M. Lambert/GI; Unit 8 Suttipong Sutiratanachai/GI; Rebecca Yale/GI; Ivan Cano/GI; By Marc Guitard/GI; by Marc Guitard/GI; DEA/G. SIOEN/GI; Majority World/GI; Pawel Opaska/GI; Pawel Opaska/GI; Getty Images/GI; David Marsden/GI; Dendeimos/GI; kozyrskyi/GI; Eduardo Fonseca Arraes/GI; Mohd Haniff Abas/GI; AFP/GI; Arun Roisri/GI; Ghislain & Marie David De Lossy/GI; lunamarina/Shutterstock; dawnanderson419/GI; KTSDESIGN/GI; Rebecca Yale/GI; kozyrskyi/GI; Harry Collins/GI; Unit 9 Carolyn Cole/GI; Wang He/GI; Javier Zayas/GI; Arthur Morris/GI; acceptfoto/GI; KeithSzafranski/GI; Chase Dekker Wild-Life Images/GI; Westend61/GI; Gado Images/GI; Mark Hamblin/GI; fototrav/GI; Juan Buitrago/GI; Giordano Cipriani/GI; Mark Webster/GI; Tim Graham/GI; Remanz/GI; Westend61/GI; George Karbus Photography/GI; Mike Brinson/GI; Shene/GI; track5/GI; George Karbus Photography/GI; Mike Brinson/GI; Shene/GI; Track5/GI; ROMEO GACAD/GI; Godong/GI; TOBIAS SCHWARZ/GI; Istvan Kadar Photography/GI; Vicki Jauron, Babylon and Beyond Photography/GI; Istvan Kadar Photography/GI; Vicki Jauron, Bab lon And Beond Photography/GI; JLewisPhoto/GI; Rob Maynard/GI; Rob Maynard/GI; Paul Souders/GI; SolStock/GI; Iaroshenko/GI; kiszon pascal/GI; Mike Hill/GI; SolStock/GI; Westend61/GI; kali9/GI

Key: GI= Getty Images

Development of this publication has made use of the Cambridge English Corpus (CEC). The CEC is a multi-billion word computer database of contemporary spoken and written English. It includes British English, American English and other varieties of English. It also includes the Cambridge Learner Corpus, developed in collaboration with Cambridge Assessment English. Cambridge University Press has built up the CEC to provide evidence about language use that helps to produce better language teaching materials.